THIS IS
COACHING

PRAISE

"Excellent! *This is Coaching* offers a unique and powerful approach to leadership coaching fundamentals. A guide for new and seasoned coaches alike, Matt's practical advice and relevant research is for anyone wanting profound and lasting results with their clients."

— DR. MARSHALL GOLDSMITH - *Thinkers50* #1
Executive Coach and *New York Times* bestselling author
of *The Earned Life, Triggers,* and
What Got You Here Won't Get You There

"A book on coaching is challenging, like a book on jazz improv. It has to capture the power and nuance of the topic; it has to take a stand without being formulaic. Matt nails it, with a balanced mix of practical advice and rich, evocative metaphors that convey the feeling and spirit of coaching."

— KEN BLACKMAN - Relationship Coach

"Clients might break your heart (from the book), but Matt won't with his incisive, comprehensive and pragmatic approach to becoming the best coach, leader, and version of you."

— JOSEPH JAFFE - Host of business talk show, *Joseph Jaffe is not Famous,* and author of five books, including *Built to Suck*

"*This Is Coaching* is one of those rare books that you can pick up and read from cover to cover, or pick up and open to a random page, each time finding something new and meaningful to precisely whatever moment you're living. Wherever you find yourself on your journey as coach and as client, Matt shares honestly and clearly what he's learned and what he's still learning about how to commit to being of service and finding our way forward on this shared adventure."

— BAY LEBLANC QUINEY - Executive Coach

"Brilliant! This book lifted me right out of the weeds of my coaching and brought me back to basics in the best possible way. *This is Coaching* gave me renewed access to the wisdom and whimsy that sows the seeds of transformation. Truly a breath of fresh air!"

— SANDY TAYLOR - Head of Coaching
at Pilea Integrative Leadership

"I have been working as a coach for 6-7 years and have had extensive coach training (currently a PCC with the ICF). And there was a lot I took away from this book that I look forward to integrating into my practice. Matt includes a lot of questions that I had not considered before, and that I know will have impact with my clients. If you are a leader that wants to support your team members in creating transformation for themselves and their organizations, read this book. And then put the wisdom nuggets it holds into practice!"

— CORY MCGOWAN- Founder/Head Coach of
Adventure Partner in Minakami, Japan

"So often we try to overcomplicate things in our effort to serve our clients and seeing the simple way Matt lays out the work serves as a relieving reminder of what our jobs are. Whether you're a brand-new coach or a veteran, I highly recommend this book."

— BRIAN WANG - Startup Executive Coach

"I see this book as powerful for the new coach, who's looking to accelerate their learning and growth while gaining comfort and confidence with the craft. And also powerful for the experienced coach, who's looking to work on the fundamentals (which, btw, all the greats in any domain do!) and want a ripe context to do so. I would've loved to have this book on my bookshelf when I first started my coaching business."

— PATRICK BUGGY - Director of Operations at Heroic

"I highly recommend this as a resource to keep on hand and come back to. Whether you're a new coach or have decades of experience, there is much to learn from the wisdom in this book."

— KELBY L. KUPERSMID - Founder
and Social Impact Coach

"This is the book he wished he'd had earlier in his journey, and while it's a great book for the beginner coach, I think it's actually best seen as a reference book for coaches at *all* levels, full of useful nuggets for us. Well worth adding to your library, IMO."

— STEVE MCCREADY- Coach and
Host of *Paradoxical* Podcast

"Matt's knowledge, wisdom, and insight into the coaching industry is unmatched. He eloquently combines actionable ideas with powerful examples while taking you on a journey through your mind. Coach or not, this book will open your eyes to new beliefs and point you in the direction of aligning with your best self."

— KEVIN WATHEY - Business Growth Consultant

"A must-read for anyone interested in the art and science of coaching. With his engaging style, insightful wisdom, and practical tools, Matt's book will help readers enhance their coaching skills and deepen their impact on clients. Highly recommended!"

— TONY MARTIGNETTI - Leadership Coach,
Founder, Inspired Purpose Coaching,
Author of *Climbing the Right Mountain*

"*This is Coaching* is an excellent resource for anyone interested in becoming a coach or enhancing their coaching skills. Matt's extensive experience in the field shines through in his comprehensive approach and practical advice. This book is a must-read for anyone who wants to help others through coaching."

— DAMIAN G. ZIKAKIS - Executive Coach, Gallup-certified Strengths Coach at DGZ Coaching

"Matt is the type of coach who practices with profound love and cutting clarity what he preaches. If he's sharing an insight or recommending a tool, it's because he's tried, tested, and refined it personally first. I highly recommend learning from his lived wisdom he generously shares with the world."

— JACLYN VOUTHOURIS

"This book is filled with gut-level honesty of what you'll go through as a coach... and what is possible. He not only gives you insights into the practice of coaching, he invites you into the reality of you as coach — what you will face and address within so that you can be impactful and powerful without. If you're already a coach wanting to improve or a coach in the making, this book will light the path and give you a clearer, easier journey."

— ANGUS NELSON - CEO of EvolveMen
Leadership, Executive Strategist

"A comprehensive guide to the profession, not from the perspective of 'right answers you need to follow,' but from the perspective of a master coach helping you find your own way through the uncertainty. If you're getting started with coaching, you should start this book."

— RYAN VAUGHN - Coach / Founder
at Inside-Out Leadership

"If you're a coach or a leader feeling stuck, this book is for you. Matt strikes the perfect balance between high level theory and tactical practices for immediate application. In just 200 pages, this book helped me anchor back in the core principles of coaching, expand my communication toolkit, and re-energize my practice."

— ANNIE GAROFALO - Co-Founder
Relationship Coach at Confidante

"This book is a must read for serious coaches."

— JEFF RIDDLE - Executive coach, Reboot

"So many coaching books simply present a model and instruct the reader to push their clients through it, regardless of who either the coach or client actually is. *This Is Coaching* takes the humans in the equation deeply into consideration. Rather than presenting a model to be executed, I'd say this book offers a clear and holistic picture of how to do what all of us coaches most want to do: help our clients change their lives."

— ROTH HERRLINGER - Executive Coach and Advisor

"Matt Thieleman did something really cool with *This is Coaching*. There are plenty of books on building a coaching business, coaching style and technique, but few have explored what it's like being a coach and how to NAVIGATE a connected relationship with the client. Matt fills that gap with invaluable insights and tools."

— MARK SILVERMAN - Executive Coach, Author of *Only 10s 2.0*, Host of *The Rising Leader* Podcast

"This book reveals the simplicity of coaching without losing any of its brilliance or depth. Matt shows his ability to be both a skillful teacher and lifelong student all at once. Most coaching books can feel like eating a five course meal that leaves you overfull, this is like a collection of coaching tapas brilliance. Each bite is full of flavor, and just enough for you to learn and grow as a coach. Even if you only read a handful of the coaching nuggets in this book, it would be enough for you to learn and improve for years to come."

— TOKU MCCREE - Executive Coach & Founder of coachingMBA

"This isn't a book to be read. It's a book to be lived into."

— JACK BENNETT - Partner and COO of CultureSync

"This book isn't just for coaches. It's for leaders. It's for anyone who wants to learn how to handle the often messy and deeply life-giving experience of relating to (and being in relationships with) other humans with love, truth, courage and integrity. *This is Coaching* is a brilliantly practical handbook for creating what we want to see more of in real-time. A must-read. I'll be recommending it to my friends, family & coaching clients alike!"

— RACHEL CLIFTON - Entrepreneur and Founder of Rachel as a Service (RaaS)

"*This is Coaching* takes an unconventional approach to coaching, using relatable anecdotes and comparisons that make it easy to understand and apply to real-life situations. The book is concise yet impactful, and it is perfect for anyone who wants to gain practical insights on coaching."

— KRISTEN MASHBURN - Founder and Company Culture Consultant, KPMashburn, LLC

"I've been on a personal exploration of the coaching world this year, and this book hit a home run for me. I don't want to become a coach for my profession, but I've realized we all are coaches in one way or another. And as a leader of a business, these skills can be valuable. This collection of insights and gems can help refine how we approach supporting and leading others. Overall, I would highly recommend this book to anyone who is interested in becoming a better coach, leader, or communicator."

— MICHAEL POTTERN - Founder of Find My Zen

THIS IS
COACHING

How to Transform a
Client's Performance,
Life & Business as a
Master Coach &
Warrior of Love

MATT
THIELEMAN

gullinbursti press

For information about special discounts for bulk
purchases or author interviews, appearances, and
speaking engagements please contact:

Matt@GoldenBristle.com

First Edition

ISBN hardcover: 979-8-9877329-2-2
ISBN softcover: 979-8-9877329-0-8
ISBN ebook: 979-8-9877329-1-5

Library of Congress Control Number: 2023906102

Edited by Christina DeBusk
Development & Book Design by Rodney Miles
Cover design and launch marketing by The Hedy Society

Fahre fort, übe nicht allein die Kunst, sondern dringe auch in ihr Inneres; sie verdient es. Denn nur die Kunst und die Wissenschaft erhöhen den Menschen bis zur Gottheit.

"Do not only practice your art, but force your way into its secrets; she deserves that, for only art and knowledge can raise man to the Divine."

- Ludwig van Beethoven

This book is dedicated to us.
All of us.
We are the music makers.
And we are the dreamers of dreams.

CONTENTS

THIS IS COACHING

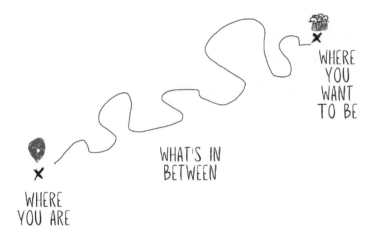

WHERE
YOU
WANT
TO BE

WHAT'S IN
BETWEEN

WHERE
YOU ARE

Download all of the illustrations and tools from this book at
www.goldenbristle.com/bookresources.

WELCOME

YESTERDAY, on the advice of my book team, I spent the afternoon dropping into nearly a dozen bookstores around Denver for book research and inspiration. And, indeed, I learned a great deal. In every store, I asked where to find a book on how to coach or on the subject of transformational coaching. And in every store, I was met with quizzical responses:

"Self-help?"

"Business?"

"Psychology?"

"Spiritual?"

"Do you mean *sports* coaching?"

At least twice, I was asked if I had checked Google or Amazon. (So much for shopping local.) And then came my favorite answer, from the owner of a new age store I was certain would have something for people who aspire to deepen their coaching:

"We have a bunch of books on personal growth. Don't people just read those and call themselves a coach? You know, everyone is just popping up as a coach these days."

In a sentence, she described why I've spent the last few months of my life writing this book, and why one of my missions in life is for everyone who calls themselves a coach to be masterful at the craft. My hope is that one day, a bookshop owner will, without hesitation, direct someone to this book when asked where they can find a resource on becoming a great coach. Later on, I'll share more about that vision and why I believe it's so important — In fact I'm excited for you to be a co-conspirator in its creation. My hope is that you feel similarly and that's what drew you to this book. But I want to invite you inward for a moment.

You picked this book for a reason. What is it? Perhaps you already have a clear answer, an image of what you hope will change for you? Perhaps it's still a feeling without words to match at this point?

Take a few seconds to write down what you'd like to get out of reading this book.

- How do you imagine you might apply the lessons to your life or coaching practice?

- If some magical outcome could occur such that everything in your life was different after this book, what would it be?

- At the very least, make a mental note of your intention for *today*. What are you looking for and how will you know you've found it?

Now, let all of that go and let's go for a ride.

– MATT THIELEMAN
December 11, 2022
Denver, Colorado

xxvi

INTRODUCTION

WHO I AM AND HOW I GOT HERE

I didn't plan to become a coach. In fact, I had no idea what coaching even was for years into my career. At best, I thought coaches were high-paid consultants who offered sage advice based on some mythical experience. At worst, I pegged them as motivational speakers of little substance and lots of fluff who charged loads of money for sparse results. That had me both put them on a pedestal of admiration and judge the hell out of them. That was my view, at least, until someone asked me to coach them and I said yes. It was a yes that changed the trajectory of my life and hopefully the lives of many people yet to come.

I grew up in a solidly middle-class family just outside of Detroit. My childhood was a wondrous mix of dark and light: deep family pain and dysfunction, love and resilience, accolades and disappointment, and struggle to both find belonging and to separate. I was one of those kids who said stuff he was too young to know about, wise beyond my years, as they say. Mythology and Eastern religions fascinated me and I could immerse myself in their stories with ease. I was intensely focused on understanding why people do what they do. On the surface, life was what others might dream up — I was high school valedictorian, a successful athlete, and generally well-liked — but I struggled to really know who I was. The titles and accolades were expected, so much that they didn't feel much like accomplishments when I achieved them. It felt as if people saw me for what I accomplished but often missed the depth of me underneath. I often felt lonely even when I was in the company of others, wondering what was missing in me or the world that would let me relax and be okay. It often felt scary for me to share myself openly for fear I'd scare others away, so my conversations stayed on the surface even as I craved more depth and openness. I wanted something different but had no idea how to get there. It was as if many parts of my life were in contradiction. Looking back, I see how every step paved the way for who I am and what I do today.

My first career was as a marketer, and coming from an education in psychology and sociology, it seemed the way I could apply my skills in the world. I also thought that power and money were requirements to make an impact in the world, and marketing was the shortest route I could see to get there. My entry into the job world coincided both with the 2008 financial crisis and the launch of a number of today's social media giants. I was good at talking with people *as human beings*, so I was well equipped for the new terrain of social and digital marketing entering our world.

It was in that world that I began to see what I call the *broken leadership styles* operating in many organizations today. The proverbial shit ran straight downhill to me as my clients unloaded their toxic cultures onto my head. Eventually, I could no longer tolerate working for companies run purely for profit, or building advertisements designed to suck attention away from other people and towards our phones.

In true entrepreneur fashion, I decided to start teaching on meditation and mindfulness without ever having meditated. Somewhere inside, I knew the practice of returning inward was key to transforming so much of the ugliness I saw in business and in the world. Fast forward a couple of years, I quit my job as a marketer, began speaking on mindful leadership, and was — suddenly — asked to coach people. (I literally Googled "How do I onboard a coaching client" before my first coaching call.)

Turns out, I was naturally quite a good coach, even without formal training or certification. To discover more of my identity as a coach, I enrolled in the Samurai Coaching

Dojo, which was a life-changing decision. It was there that I saw that coaching could be so many different things.

I also quickly noticed the common pitfalls both new and seasoned coaches continued to fall into; the ways in which our own fears, stories, and judgments get in the way of our ability to coach powerfully; and the simple (not always easy) steps that can bring us back to supporting our clients exactly where they are.

As the possibility I saw through coaching grew, so did my ambitions for its impact in the world and the clarity of my mission. Today, I am committed to a few seemingly impossible goals:

1. **To connect a coach to every founder in the world.**
   Looking at the next 50 years of leadership, I see the
   need for masterful coaches supporting the founders
   and leaders of the next generation of companies —
   early-stage startups. If we can support mindful
   leaders in creating positive cultures when they have 5
   or 50 employees instead of 500, our world will change
   massively for the better. In support of this, I spent a
   year as CEO of Pilea, a coaching network committed
   to bringing coaching support to venture-backed
   founders and their teams. During my year there, we
   built out an incredible coach community, training,
   and support to move toward that goal.

2. **For every coach in the world to be masterful at the
   craft.** Having a coach for every founder isn't worth
   much if those coaches aren't doing powerful work.
   Our work changes lives and changes the world. This
   mission inspired me to co-lead the Samurai Coaching
   Dojo after my training and heavily influenced the

work I did to build an incredible coach ecosystem at Pilea. It's also the motivation for this book. My stand for every coach in the world to be masterful at their craft is a powerful driver in my life.

3. **And my ultimate vision: A world in which every human has the skills and being of a coach**. You'll read more about this shortly. We're here for joy. We're here to express our soul. Let's keep moving towards that.

My work is a reflection of these missions: supporting coaches, supporting people in sharing their soul's work, and sharing the movement to get founders the support they need to build amazing businesses. If you want to learn more about how that looks in practice, visit https://goldenbristle.com.

WHO THIS IS FOR AND WHAT YOU'LL GET

I also didn't plan to write this book. The truth is, I woke up around 4 a.m. the last morning of a trip to Hawaii, as I was transitioning back from CEO life to coach life, and this book was, well, channeled through me. In the dark of my bedroom, I saw the sections, headlines, flow, and structure all at once. A quiet voice told me I was *publishing a book within the year*. When I arrived at the airport, I wrote about 80 percent of the outline and started writing content the day after we got home. It wasn't until later that I realized what I was actually doing and who I was doing it for.

I told you that even as a baby coach, I could spot the pitfalls most every coach fell into. That doesn't mean I didn't fall into them myself. I did and I still do. It does mean, however, that I found ways to unhook myself and quickly developed tools to use in places other coaches got stuck.

My client work went deep quickly. In short order, I emerged as a leader in the coach communities I was a part of. Clients were drawn to me over coaches who'd been in this work for years. And in my work, I was adding my own nuance to the fundamentals — making them my own while honoring the spirit of what they taught. So the lessons in this book weren't gained from any lectures, textbooks, or esoteric trainings on coaching. They aren't just psychological theory or academic research. Every insight and distinction in this book was well-earned and hard-fought in my own work as a coach and as a client. They came from stumbles, mistakes, leaps of faith, and rounds and rounds of practice — messy, courageous, and full-contact. And they came directly from some of the master coaches I've had the pleasure of learning from and working alongside over the years. This is coaching in practice, not just theory.

- At first glance, the contents of this book might appear quite basic. It might look like it's for brand-new coaches or people just now thinking about coaching. That's (sort of) true. *This book is for you if you want to know and understand the basics of coaching.* That includes people who want to improve their leadership and ability to inspire people to do their best work. But that isn't the only group this book is for.

INTRODUCTION

- Whether you've been coaching for 2 days or 20 years, if you believe your work starts with you, this book has something to offer. Don't be fooled by your first take. The lessons herein will take you deeper with yourself and your clients, *if you apply them*. Maybe you've found your clients stagnating or yourself growing a bit bored. Dive into these tools and see what they unlock.

- Lastly, this book might also be for you if you're a therapist or mental health professional curious about how you might fit coaching into your work (from my perspective). Some of my favorite work is in supporting therapists to step outside of the constraints of therapy and into coaching.

After reading this, I believe you'll walk away with a better awareness of yourself as a coach and human, which will in turn allow you to see your clients more fully as they are. I also believe you'll gain useful tools that you can apply immediately to support your clients in bridging the gap between where they are right now and where they want to be.

Worst case, what I offer is old hat and you leave with a greater confidence in your own knowledge and abilities, which might have you take more risks in service of your clients' transformation. Best case, you'll have an entirely new model for supporting growth that sends both your life and your clients' lives toward exponential joy and success. Either way, reading this book has the power to transform you as a coach and leader in the world. I hope you'll choose to allow that.

MY CALL TO YOU

There is a vision in my mind. It's still quite blurry, still incubating and coming to light. It's the vision of a transforming and transformed world. In it, every person has the skills, tools, and ways of being of a coach. It's a world of courageous conversations, emotional expression, creative freedom, and deep love. And it starts with how we choose to relate to and communicate with each other.

Coaching is an extremely powerful force when put to good use. It sheds light on what is otherwise dark, opens doors we've closed without knowing, reveals strengths and abilities we've long forgotten, and provides a sense of belonging in the times we struggle to find it. Coaching can connect us to our humanity and divinity all at once, helping us to forge a new version of ourselves, more curious and capable and confident. It can also be quite painful as we dissolve our old self in the process of creating anew.

Coaching is a big fucking deal.

If my vision — a world in which everyone has the tools and the being of a coach — is to come to life, we have to be able to articulate what the heck coaching even is. We could probably use a legion of masterful coaches committed to the craft and to sharing the message. And we might also benefit from some simple tools for practicing or teaching coaching to newcomers.

Since you're here, you're part of that legion. A warrior of love. I hope this book aids you in your journey and becomes a trusty tool in your toolkit. More than anything, I hope it inspires you to continue to walk the path of your own personal transformation, to share your light with the world, and to invite others to join the cause.

INTRODUCTION

PART ONE:

THE PROMISE

OF COACHING

COACHING IS GPS NAVIGATION: PART ONE: NAVIGATING OUR LIFE

IMAGINE YOU'RE IN your car ready to drive somewhere you've never been before. You open up the map app on your phone and it offers you a known set of steps to get driving directions. The first thing it shows you is a little dot of your current location. You click a button to get directions and it asks you where you want to go. Finally, you hit navigate and it shares step-by-step instructions on what to do to get where you want.

Your GPS gives you three critical things:

- where you are

- where you want to go

- and the steps along the way.

Now imagine a different experience with your friendly GPS app. You open it and it asks you how you're doing, then waits for your response. Instead of having you choose a destination, it just starts telling you to turn left, then right, then drive straight. You ask the app where it's taking you and it says, "Where you want to go."

But where is that? And how does it think it knows?

Unfortunately, that's how way too many coaching conversations go. Coaches so badly want their clients to leave feeling better or with some sort of insight that they start "coaching" without knowing where they're headed or why. It's the trap of being someone who wants to help others. It comes from a well-intentioned place but left unchecked, it's like getting directions to an unknown destination. It might feel fun and you might end up somewhere exciting, but you might as well be running in circles.

We're going to continue this analogy of coaching as GPS navigation throughout this book, using it as a framework on which to build a set of tools. I find it's a concept people who have never been coached can relate to and an effective way for them to understand the experience. Even better, it reminds me of my job as a coach so that when I sit with clients, I don't act like the weird app just giving random directions.

The trick is, the GPS framework is deceptively simple. It's only three steps, but each of the steps is infinitely expansive and nuanced. They never end — for our clients or for us. That's the joy of being a coach. We get to spend our entire lives going deeper and deeper into this work, knowing that it's never done.

We'll start with the two necessary components for effective directions:

- where you are now

- and where you want to go.

The funny thing about human behavior compared to map directions is that these two are often intertwined. We consider where we want to be in relation to where we are right now, and vice versa. As such, the teachings in those chapters may seem at times like they bounce back and forth. I'm simply relaying my experience as both a coach and a client when getting clear on those two things.

There is an inherent tension and dance between where we are and where we want to be. It's challenging to identify what we really want without being able to rest exactly where we are right now. Similarly, spending too much time looking at where we are can get in the way of looking at what we want instead. So, we dance. And, so, I've danced as I've written what comes next. I invite you to move to the music along with me. The majority of our time will be spent on these first two components because this is where the heavy lifting happens in coaching. Most shifts occur as we learn to clearly ask for what we really want and get really honest with where we are right now. That's powerful coaching.

The final section — what's along the way — is probably what you imagine is most of the coaching process (that's what I thought). Don't rush there. Allow the lessons herein to unfold as intended. You'll notice that by the time you get there, most of the coaching has already happened along the way.

A warm welcome as you embark on this adventure

Welcome, fellow traveler. It's great to meet someone else on this path. What path, you ask? Well, the one you stepped onto the minute you decided you were a coach. (If you consider yourself a leader, you're a coach. Better get used to it now. It'll make the rest of our time together much more fun.)

Of course, you can step off the path if you'd like. But I don't think that's the game you're here to play. So then, what game(s) are you playing?

The game of coaching as a spiritual journey.

The game of growth.

The game of discovery.

The game of moving closer to yourself in service of love.

Those are the games a coach plays. Here are some of the rules of engagement I've picked up along the way. Feel free to add your own to the mix:

- You get to challenge everything you believe to be true — about yourself, about others, about the world, and about life.

- You get to be wrong (a lot!). And you get to choose how you relate to that. You get to choose what it means about you, if anything.

- You get to choose your worth and worthiness. (I hope you choose to accept and embrace it.)

- You get to face your demons, your stories, your younger selves, your various parts, your integrated whole, your shadows and blind spots, and your perceived failures and victories.

- You get to let go of all of these. Or keep them. It's your choice!

- You get to get triggered. You get to choose what happens next.

- You get to choose how big you dream, what's possible for you, and what's not. You get to choose where you're going and how you want to get there.

- You get to choose your companions (or lack thereof) along the way.

- You get to choose what success means for you. You get to choose what it doesn't mean, too. You even get to choose *if* success is a measure in your life.

- You get to choose if *anything* is a measure in your life.

- You get to choose how you spend your days, weeks, months, and years.

- You get to choose how much of your love, power, brilliance, wisdom, creativity, joy, and passion you show to the world.

- You get to choose how much love, power, brilliance, wisdom, creativity, joy, and passion you let in from the world.

- You get to choose what you stand for, what you value.

- You get to choose what you're a Yes to and what you're a No to. You get to choose how you share those with the world.

- You get to choose how you respond to the world's response.

- You get to choose to grow.

- You get to choose to push. You get to choose to rest.

- You get to choose to be courageous.

- You get to cheat as much as you want. You get to choose what counts as cheating, too, and how you treat people who cheat.

- You get to win. You get to lose. You get to choose what both of those mean. (I hope you win!)

- You get to choose what any of your choices above — and so many more — mean about you, the world, and the people around you.

- Most importantly, you get to remember that you're God*. And you get to choose what that means for you.

I'm sure there are more. Oh, and you can take them or leave them as you'd like. It's your choice after all.

(*Make this word mean whatever you want it to mean. More than anything, I'm referring to the force that creates, binds, holds, and gives life to everything. I often call it Love. I'm not here to debate or press a religious agenda. Let your unique divinity speak for itself.)

ON COACHING

My philosophy of coaching has emerged from a deeply held belief: that we were designed for growth. It's in our biological and spiritual nature, baked into who we are. We seek out knowledge, insights, and awareness about ourselves and the world often simply for the sake of learning. We seek new. We want novelty (even as we try to hold onto what we have). That's being human. And it can sometimes be invisible to us.

As coaches, we get the privilege and honor of witnessing our clients grow first-hand, including the victories and struggles along the way. All the while, we also get to grow into a new version of ourselves, ever-better equipped to be the support our clients need on their journey.

What is coaching? It's difficult to speak to it in a single sentence.

- Coaching is an act of love and service, to ourselves, our clients, and the world.

- Coaching is living from a particular way of being, some of which is captured throughout this book.

- Coaching is an inquiry into what's possible, who we are, and what either of those things even means.

From our clients' perspectives, I think my friend Toku McCree nailed the definition of coaching quite succinctly:

Coaching is helping someone to have the life they want while becoming more of themselves.

That's the perfect setup for the rest of this book. If we, as coaches, come from a place where people are growing and want to get somewhere in their life, we're pretty set.

Now onto the nuts and bolts.

WHAT HAPPENS IN A COACHING CONVERSATION

When we think of the coaching toolbox, the most commonly used item is the *coaching conversation*. Conversation is where the proverbial coaching magic happens. In the span of a few minutes to a few hours, we get to walk alongside our clients as they move through the process of identifying what they want, where they are now, and what sits along the way.

During that journey, any number of things might happen. Feelings might arise, new dreams might emerge, and planning and preparation might result.

I can't tell you exactly what happens in a coaching conversation. If I tried right now, I'd be writing myself into a corner. Instead, after this little bit of level-setting, what I'll do is offer my best guidance on how to set up the conditions for said magic that I believe is a natural byproduct of great coaching.

Coaching helps us to create a new world, a new life that was just waiting to be imagined, a more complete version of ourselves.

That's what we're doing. That's what happens. How do we get there? Well, that is best experienced in the moment.

WHAT IS THE PURPOSE OF A COACHING CONVERSATION?

Let's ground ourselves more firmly into what I'm speaking of when I make the statements above, and let's break down some common aspects of coaching conversations.

Afterword, we can get into talk of magic and spirit discovery and that fun stuff.

Tangibly, four things generally exist in every coaching conversation and, I would assert, are a requirement for deep transformation. They are *empowerment, possibility, enrollment,* and *commitment.*

Empowerment

Clients become empowered to create their own lives from their desires and dreams. Through the inquiry and guidance of a coach, they have the chance to spot the places in their life they're playing a victim or letting others decide their choices for them.

As they choose empowerment in more parts of their life, things spiral upward and more freedom comes their way.

Possibility

As clients choose to create something new in life, possibility emerges. It's the idea that something else might be available. Something outside the scope of their current life or worldview. Something that felt out of their reach until now.

With possibility comes fear. Fear this might not work. Fear of losing the thing they imagined before even getting it. Fear of losing what they have now as they grow.

Possibility and fear are traveling companions on this journey.

Enrollment

To realize this new possibility, new beliefs and actions are likely required. When clients are enrolled in the positive benefits of what they want and their own power to create it, they are more likely to shift those actions. They have to at least be open to believing in themselves in order to transform.

Commitment

This is where the rubber meets the road. Commitment is coming from the place in which their vision is already true and acting accordingly. It's returning to empowerment, possibility, and enrollment over and over again on the way up the mountain.

As coaches, we have a massive set of tools at our disposal to support clients in this process, some of which include:

- Deep inquiry
- Role play
- Somatic experience
- Reflection and mirroring
- Teaching
- Problem-solving
- Accountability
- Motivation

- Goal-setting

Whichever of these you want to wield, or any others, have at it. Just know that any one tool is not what coaching is. Coaching is not something that is so easily contained.

COACHING IS A JOURNEY

It's a journey for you and your client — in some direction, with intention, together.

It's a process of discovery — of what works and what doesn't, what's helpful and what isn't, what's real and what's imagined. Most importantly, it's a discovery of your client's hidden strength and divine truth.

As far as I know, only two things are constant:

1. There is no right way.
2. You don't get to know what happens.

And with that, off you go along your way.

COACHING IS A SPIRITUAL PRACTICE

When you signed up for this strange little lifetime as a human, you made a cosmic agreement: You would forget that you're God.

You also agreed to forget that you signed the agreement. We all signed this silly agreement. And it has a bunch of silly downstream effects that cause us to do silly things and act in silly ways.

So when your clients (or you) show up and play small, don't ask for what they want, complain about stuff in their control, play victim to their circumstances, avoid the practices they've committed to, or do any number of things to sabotage themselves, just remember: They've merely forgotten who they are. That's why they have you.

As coaches, we get to remember and re-remember the truth. Divine love, wisdom, integrity, joy, abundance, and love (again) flow through us all the time, in every way. We cannot escape it, despite our faulty memory. We get to continue to move closer to our true nature with every client, every mistake, every breakdown and breakthrough, and every choice we make in our lives.

Of course, walking this path is not a requirement for being a human. You can choose *out* just as easily as you can choose *in*. But you chose *in*. You're a coach. So this is what we're doing. Welcome.

When you invite your clients to consider what they want, you're speaking to their divine creativity and desire. When you choose to be a stand for them having the thing they want, you're relating to their divine power. When you lovingly challenge their old patterns, you're calling forth their divine wisdom, love, and grace. When you hold space for their emotions and breakdowns, you're giving love to their divine child and wounding.

As you see them in this way — their divinity rather than their fears — you create room for them to heal. You're dispelling the human fog that tells them they're separate. You're showing them their own *godness*.

23

And in doing so, you heal yourself. You see through your own fog. You tap into your own divinity. God seeing God. One recognizing itself in another. That's why we're all here.

COACHING IS A FULL-CONTACT SPORT

Being a coach means being committed to:

- Supporting clients in getting somewhere they've never been before
- Supporting them in shifting everything standing in their way of getting what they want
- Shifting everything standing in your own way of getting what your clients want
- Living the life of a coach, leader, and transformational being
- Seeing what's possible and standing for its existence, even in the darkest of times
- Loving what is along the way

It's the most wonderful (literally full of wonder), creative, jaw-droppingly beautiful job in the world. It's a gift to be able to bring that commitment to others. And it requires everything you've got. You're playing on the razor's edge. You're the (wo)man in the arena, marred by dust and blood. You and your client both are daring greatly when you sign up for this work.

There is no hiding when you're supporting others to transform. There is no playing it safe when you're creating the impossible. That doesn't mean it has to be hard. The suffering is optional, even if the growth is not.

YOU ARE A GUEST HOUSE

You can rest assured that your client's survival mechanisms, resistance, ego habits, and self-sabotaging patterns are going to come out. They're doing what they do: trying to keep themselves in the safety of their known bubble.

And if you're doing it right, your same patterns are going to come out, too, because you'll be working with clients who challenge you to show up at your best.

- If you're a people pleaser, your client will question your love for them.

- If you're a perfectionist, your client will point out the missteps in your process.

- If you're triggered by anger, your client will unleash a rageful storm on you.

- If your client's breakthrough is to stop thinking so much, you'll start thinking about how much they're thinking.

- If your client is creating a money breakthrough, your money patterns will hit you full force.

Your job is to remain in the fray (holding boundaries, of course), no matter what your client brings, holding the door open to what else is possible for them. And your job is to spot your own patterns as they emerge, continuing in your own work to integrate them.

Welcome and entertain them all. They are guides from beyond, appearing to accompany you and your client along the path of transformation.

YOUR CLIENT'S JOURNEY IS YOUR JOURNEY

When I'm struggling — in my own development and with my clients — a common phrase comes out of my mouth when I talk to *my* coach: "I just shared this lesson with my client." And there isn't a month that goes by without me muttering it. I'm entirely okay with that (right now, at least, though I am less excited in the moment). It means that my clients are up to big things and I'm participating in my growth alongside them.

A couple of years ago, I started tracking (as you'll see in a few pages) what my growth opportunity would be with each new client I met. During my first call with a potential client, I now challenge myself to spot the breakthrough that they, as my client, are helping me to create. It's a forcing function of sorts (I love those). And it invites me to look deeper at these questions for both of us:

- What about their vision scares me?
- What do I believe isn't possible?
- What part of their path am I assuming will be hard?
- Where am I inventing pitfalls that aren't there?
- How do I want them to change?

- What parts of them am I not accepting and loving right now?

- What parts of them do I admire or pretend I don't have?

- How am I putting them (or me) on a pedestal?

As I dig into these questions, I get to see my own growth opportunities. I get to bring light to the parts of myself I've obscured or tried to avoid. I get to engage in my own coaching process:

- Where am I now, really?

- Where do I want to be with a particular thing?

- What is in the way right now?

With that, my client and I are now walking parallel paths, not only on their journey but on my own. When I reach my edge in our work, I get to take responsibility for it and get back to focusing on my client. So it is for both of us.

YOU'RE CREATING THE IMPOSSIBLE

When someone signs on to work with you, they're signing on to create something entirely new in their life and in the world. It's like they have two lives (one before coaching and one after coaching) that diverge in wonderful and unpredictable ways.

Your clients are never the same, even if nothing on the outside changes.

27

The intervention of coaching is creating the impossible. If what your client wanted was possible for them in their current world, they'd already have it. And it will be impossible until the moment it arrives, never sooner.

You're helping your clients identify and choose the games they're playing, with new rules and better prizes. If they were playing Monopoly and the highest bill was worth $500, when the two of you make a $5,000 bill, what's possible in that game changes. Suddenly, the upper limit for their bank account has skyrocketed. Hotels are available on every property. Or maybe they decide it's now a cooperative game in which everyone works together and collectively wins. Or that people sing a song instead of paying rent. Remember, they always win the game they're playing, even if they aren't sure what it is. That's the power of coaching.

Anything is possible.

A good friend asked me once what lesson I would give my child if I could pick only one. After huffing and puffing about only being asked to name one thing, I said, "You're playing a game with infinite choice. You get to pick the rules and you can't pick wrong. Most importantly, no matter what, the Universe and I will always love you."

When your client was born, they were given a menu of options for how they could expect their life to turn out. Depending on a whole host of factors, including their demographic, socioeconomic, and familial environments, the choices on that menu could range from one to several thousand. No matter what, those options are limited. Your job is to help them add to that menu.

There might be things on the menu they've personally crossed off. There might be things they've written and their parents have crossed off. There might be things they didn't know could ever be on the menu. There might be things they've always wanted to see on the menu but have been too afraid to ask for (those are my favorite).

As you walk alongside your client, adding to their menu options, something will start to happen. They'll start adding things on their own. The list will get so long that they'll need a new piece of paper to hold it all. Eventually, they'll start to see that the only thing limiting the menu was them. It was their hesitance to explore and seek and experiment and, well, ask for what they really want that kept them stuck.

Together, you'll start to understand that anything really is possible. That's the joy of being a coach.

Our clients get to teach us the lessons we already know, over and over again. They get to inspire us to add to our own menus, to believe that more is available to us than we ever imagined. And together, we get to create a virtuous cycle of magical awesomeness that creates a more beautiful world.

What was once impossible becomes possible.

For them.

And for you.

IT'S ABOUT THEM

Here's an uncomfortable truth: Your clients don't hire you for the reasons you think. Your clients do not pay you for your time. They do not pay you for your attention. They do not pay you for the fancy tools you have or your proven frameworks, for your good looks, your brilliance, your education, or your experience.

They might think they do. They might use your framework as a rationalization for their decision. They might be inspired or in awe of your accomplishments. They might see you as an expert in the thing they're struggling with. That's all great, but it's not really what's going on.

They pay you for *them*. For the life they have just a glimmer of right now and want to see and experience fully. For the feeling they'll have (or think they'll have) when their idea is realized. For the thing that pains them right now to not bring to the world.

They also pay you for the look in their partner's eyes when they commit to a lifetime together. Or for the opportunity to make the impossible possible. And paying you is proof that all of that can actually happen if they make the choice.

It's not about you. It's about them — more than that, even. It's about something *bigger* than them. They believe that something else is possible for them and for the world. They see a future with more love, abundance, joy, purpose, and impact. They see a world free from suffering. They see relationships that light people up and open their hearts. They see creativity, expression, and innovation that transforms lives.

You're just the gateway, the door opener, the companion along the path, the mirror, the light that shines back their innate greatness, and the person to love them when they fall over and fear they can't get back up.

When you show up in that way, what they hope is possible actually becomes possible — for them and for the world. None of that is about time. None of that is about a process. None of that is about you.

IT'S ALSO ABOUT YOU

Just as true: Who you *be* makes all the difference.

You might find it difficult to sell yourself as a coach because if someone says no, you'll feel rejected. You might feel afraid to shine your light too brightly because you'll dim others or put yourself in the way of criticism. You also might hesitate to speak the truth you see because you could be misunderstood. Or you might avoid sharing your struggles and humanity with others out of fear they won't trust you. All of that is true for me. And all of it is in the way of me doing my best work with my clients.

That doesn't make me a bad or ineffective coach. It makes me a human. It isn't my fault that I have limiting thoughts and behaviors. But it is my responsibility to continue to grow beyond them. That growth is in service to me, my clients, and the world.

We choose the clients we work with because their journey has something to teach us. The work challenges us to continue to deepen ourselves so we can continue to be of service. I'd say it's inescapable, but it's not.

Some coaches choose to plateau, to keep doing what they've found works and ride it out. That's a choice, too.

But that isn't you, is it?

You're here because you're called to the challenge. Your job is to move through what's in the way for you so you can help your clients reach places they've never imagined.

As you level up, so will they. As they level up, so must you.

YOUR CLIENTS WILL BREAK YOUR HEART

They will avoid seeing the possibility you hold in front of them. They will rebel against their own power and greatness. They will ask to quit when right on the verge of a huge breakthrough. Clients will back out of a committed agreement with you at the very last minute. They'll blame you or something outside of themselves for all of it. And on and on and on.

They will show up as humans. If you're standing powerfully for them, they will show up more expressed in their humanity with you than anywhere else in their life.

Sometimes you'll want to shake them until they wake up, or climb down into their hole and save them, or force them to get on a call with you. You'll want to make them see what you see no matter what it takes. None of those things is your job.

Your job is to love them and to challenge them to remember who they really are, without attaching yourself to the outcome, over and over and over again. To do that, take care of yourself. Be in your own work and growth and development. Treat yourself with love.

You've got this.

LEARN TO BE A CLIENT TO LEARN TO BE A COACH

You need a coach. You need to experience what transformation is like from your client's perspective. You need to commit money, time, and energy to something that scares you. You need to feel the feeling of being on the fence and choosing *hell YES!* or *hell NO!* to the life you've dreamed of.

You need to risk disappointing someone else when something just doesn't feel right. You need to receive 100 percent love and 100 percent challenge from someone who's not going anywhere.

You need to be a stand for what's possible in yourself if you hope to be a stand for what's possible in others.

Your money fears will show up. Your old wounds will hurt and invite you to heal them, maybe after some thrashing and avoiding. Your projections will come out in full force, insisting that everything is everyone else's fault and you can't actually do it. Your ego will grab hold of all the insights you've gained in the past and use them to try to convince you that you're done growing.

They'll challenge you every step of the way as you grow into the limitless power you possess. They'll also make you a better coach every time you learn to integrate them. That's the way through. That's the way this world changes: through our own commitment to what could be, and our willingness to move toward it.

Be a coach by being a client.

THE BEING OF A COACH

You aren't merely a human asking questions of another human or giving them space to share what's on their mind. Transformational coaching goes beyond what a lamppost or chatbot can do. It touches your client's soul and invites them to remember who they really are.

Try on different energies in your coaching. Mix and match and experiment and play. As you expand your range, your clients will expand what they call forth from you. Here are some styles for you to try on.

Be the mountain

The mountain does not move. It does not waver, flinch, steel itself, or shiver. The mountain stands tall, day and night, in the face of whatever comes its way. "I'm here," it says. And that's that.

The mountain holds a structure for life to flourish. Its soil feeds plants and beneficial organisms. It recycles decaying matter into new birth. Its curves and edges offer shelter to animals. Its rivers feed the grasses at its feet with pure water from its head and shoulders. It has room for all of this and more.

Be the blue sky

The blue sky smiles and you smile back. "I see you," it says, and you feel seen. You know it's there even on the cloudiest of days, when the dreariness seems never-ending.

You can bring its radiance into your mind anytime, lifting your spirit and calming your mind. It invites you to spread your wings and fly, soar, and weave across its limitless expanse.

The blue sky has seen it all. Devastating storms, whisps of clouds that are almost imperceptible, wondrous rainbows, and clear stillness. It is unfazed and open, ready for what's next. It loves it all. That's what it's here for.

Be the ocean

The ocean is play. It says, "Come out and explore! Come see what adventure awaits!" It also says, "Come face yourself. I promise I won't take it easy on you. You're welcome. You wouldn't want me to anyway!"

Swim, dive, dance, sing, flip, or rest all day. It's all welcome here. The world is your oyster, and the ocean is full of them.

The ocean is power. Unrelenting. Faceless and dark, clear and bright. What's one drop, one spoonful, to the ocean? Nothing. Bring it on.

The ocean is hard, hammering the earth with wave after wave. It's soft, gently seeking new ground in the tiniest of cracks. It's patient. Years are like milliseconds in the ocean's lifetime.

The ocean is creation and destruction. Life and death. It is mother and it is father, receptive womb and penetrative force. Its waters are soothing and healing. They hold us up and pull us down.

Its waves teach us life's rhythms, in and out, up and down. They remind us of the preciousness of each breath, each heartbeat, each pulse.

Be bamboo

The bamboo plant flexes and flows with the wind. Its leaves dance in celebration of the breeze, swinging and swaying at the joy of living each and every moment. When gale-force winds blow and stiff, rigid trees come crashing down, the roots of the bamboo remain intact.

When bamboo is cut, it is not phased. Instead, it regenerates faster, and so its growth rate surpasses that of other trees. It becomes antifragile, ready for anything.

Be the sun

The sun shines with a warmth and light that never dims. All day, every day (even when it's dark for half the world), the sun gifts us more than we could ever need.

Its gravitational force holds us within its arms, at the perfect distance for us to thrive. Yet, it does not strain. It trusts that what it offers is enough (and it is). For that, it lasts billions of years.

The sun's power of illumination stretches for galaxies and galaxies across the cosmos. Plants and animals seek its light as food and power. Its heat burns away what is no longer needed and clarifies what's left so we can move forward focused and true.

Be music

Music is the flow of life. At once, it creates, follows, and breaks its own rules. Music transcends divisions, unites, and calls forth peace.

Music evokes our most primal and basic natures, as well as our most elevated and divine. It heals. It opens our hearts to truth without words.

Music has no wrong notes when you're in the flow. Its rhythm carries us away, into a new world. Follow the music and you'll never be lost.

Be the divine in all forms

The mountain, sky, ocean, bamboo tree, and sun are not self-conscious. They do not worry about how they look or sound. They exist without judgment or comparison, jealousy or greed. What they are, they are, that is all.

They are whole. They are complete as they are. They do not need permission to show up and reveal their true nature. They do not worry about whether they belong, or whether they're too much, or how things might turn out. Their connection to the divine is complete.

You are already all of them and more. Rest in that truth.

NO ONE NEEDS A COACH

Just like no one needs to exercise or eat their vegetables or practice gratitude or meditate or get eight hours of sleep or shower every day or pay their rent or drink water. None of those are requirements for any of us (no matter how badly you want them to be). They do have impacts, though. Those are two different things. Your client doesn't need you.

And.

If any of us wants to get the life, impact, and results we desire with less pain and suffering...

A coach can be the way.

You have something that will save your client's life. You are the answer to their problems. You have exactly the medicine they've been searching for!

All of it is true: They don't need you *and* you have what they need.

Act like it.

No one has time or money for a coach.

Everyone is busy and full and has already allocated every dollar coming their way. They don't need to change anything.

And.

Committing time on a regular basis to lovingly conspire with the universe and create their dream life will change everything for them. Intentionally putting money or some other energy toward that commitment will kickstart the change.

(We cannot predict what those changes will be for certain.)

All of it is true: Your client doesn't have time or money and their time and money are waiting to be put to this new use.

Accept it.

Your ability to hold a multitude of truths all at once is your coach superpower. Harness it and your clients will feel like you make everything they've ever wanted possible. It's why they need you (even though they don't need you)!

ON CONTAINERS

Coaching is a process of alchemy. One thing goes in and another comes out. It is transformation and it's quite beautiful. That transformation can't happen without the right environment. A combination of empowerment, possibility, enrollment, commitment, time, attention, pressure, awareness, and more come together to produce magical outcomes that always surprise me.

That's the power of a container.

A container needs to be the right size, shape, and structure for its use.

My plants live in pots slightly larger than their roots so they have room to grow. Too large or small of a container and the plant cannot thrive. The bottoms have holes to allow for water flow. Without holes, water pools and roots begin to rot. The outsides are colorful and textured to add life to our home (and inspire me and my partner to love on them).

When I brew beer, my fermentation container is sanitized and clean. It's tightly sealed, with the exception of a one-way valve at the top that lets out air bubbles from yeast burps. If the valve doesn't work, the beer goes bad.

For pickling vegetables, I use an even tighter container. It's sealed so nothing gets in or out. The amplifying pressure allows for more chemical reactions to take place, sprouting new vitamin combinations and the growth of beneficial bacteria.

Each of those containers is designed to provide the right environment for the little beings inside of them to grow and change in the way that works best for them. My pickles wouldn't pickle in a flowerpot and my flowers would die in a pickle jar.

Building the right container for your clients is as important as any coaching work you do inside of it. Unfortunately, many coaches make two mistakes (that you're going to change now that you're reading this!):

1. We don't pay enough attention to our containers.

2. We don't make our containers strong enough.

I'm using "we" in those statements with intention because I'm guilty of this myself. I've allowed clients to slide into a coaching relationship with me without clear agreements on how we would handle last-minute cancellations or payment terms.

I've also lowered my rates to match a client's fear rather than their possibility when I've known that holding strong would have better served them. As a result, clients have quit or shown up without much power to our work. It's not on them; it's on me.

The reason many coaches don't set the appropriate container with clients is simple: fear.

This fear shows up as something like:

- "What if they say no?"

- "What if they get upset?"

- "What if I remind them of our agreements and they quit?"

- "What if I can't stick to our agreements?"

- "Talking about that would take up time we really need for coaching."

If you're just building your coaching practice or in need of money, these questions can get really loud. Coaches are afraid of how their clients will react to them holding the container, afraid that they, as coaches, won't be able to handle the reaction, so they hold back and tell themselves that it's in service of letting the client decide what to work on.

Here's the secret: *The container is the coaching.*

How they (and you) show up in the face of their commitments is relevant to every part of their life, to everything they want to create, to every future dream and vision.

It is what you're there for. And if you set powerful agreements on the strength of your container at the start, it's another tool in service of their transformation when challenges arise.

YOUR CONTAINERS AREN'T STRONG ENOUGH

Again, I know because *my* containers often aren't strong enough. It's a constant work in progress, an adjustment that's best done in partnership.

While writing this book, I've had multiple clients quit their work with me right after committing or in the middle of a long-term agreement.

It's tough. It shook me.

From those learnings, the container I now create for new clients — even as we're exploring the possibility of working together — is much stronger. I completely reworked my new client agreements and set some required practices for new clients to take on as we enter into our work. I put more attention and care into the beginning of our work, reveal more of myself, and am more clear on the game I'm inviting my clients to play. As a result, we get to go deeper more quickly.

HOW TO MAKE MORE POWERFUL CONTAINERS

Designing the containers of our coaching work is no different from the coaching process we walk our clients through. You start with the end in mind, design backward, and walk step-by-step along the way.

Step 1: Define the game you're playing

Are you growing flowers, brewing beer, or pickling vegetables? The nature of your client's (and your) desired outcome will determine the shape and texture of your container. Get clear on what you're doing this for and allow the shape of your container to follow.

My clients come to me for deep, soul transformation. So, my containers look different from those of a productivity coach. They should. Know your game and build from there.

Bonus: What game would you love to play? What coaching container and relationship would light you on fire? What agreements would be required for that to happen?

Step 2: Imagine success and ask what happened along the way

- How did you show up to your work?

- How did your client show up to your work?

- Who was each of you being?
- Who was each of you not being?

You can likely predict the ways **you** and your client will unconsciously undermine the work you're doing. Make note of those before they happen and **talk** about them. Get everything on the table that might derail your work and create a success plan together.

Step 3: Make agreements and review them together

Steve Chandler was the first coach to turn me on to making agreements instead of having expectations. Both you and your client likely have unspoken expectations of each other and yourselves entering into your work. The longer they go unspoken, the more they'll get in the way of things. Make time for both of you to opt into a certain way of showing up together.

Slow this part down. Talk about how you want to relate to the agreements, what you'll do when one of you fails to live up to them, and how you'd like to remind each other and call each other back in. Become collaborators and co-conspirators in the game of transforming your client's life.

Step 4: Review them frequently

Do this both by yourself and with your client. You can start sessions reviewing some or all of your agreements. You can ask yourself if anything feels like it's missing from your coaching container.

Invite your client to do the same. You're both building it together. Invite the energies of empowerment, possibility, enrollment, and commitment to every second you spend together.

Step 5: Break shit

Go make a mess. Have fun. Push things. Tell the truth. Allow for conflict. Rupture and repair. Then come back to your agreements and do it all again. That's what we're here for, after all.

Tool: The Exploration Questions

Use these questions to practice seeing the way forward for your clients and yourself. The point is not to get them right and hold onto them, forcing your work down the path you see. Rather, it's to practice seeing what might be there and then letting go, knowing your client has all the wisdom they need to find the right way.

During your first exploration call with a client, put these bullets at the top of your notes. During the call, jot down what you think might fall under each of them. Continue to refer to them during your work together, checking against your initial instinct.

- Wants
- Needs
- Their breakthrough
- My breakthrough

You'll notice none of these point to things in the way or explain why what they want can't happen. That's not what you're focused on here. You're focused on where you are going and what positive shifts you imagine will happen along the way. You're creating a new future with these notes, for you and your client.

What do they want?

The answer to this question comes directly from your client. It's why they report coming to you in the first place. It's the thing they think is missing in their life and/or the strategy they've identified to get it.

This is the first question on the list because it's the first question a coach ought to be thinking about every time they meet a client. That's also why it happens to be the first part of the coaching framework in this book.

Your job is not to filter their answers when taking notes on this but to capture as accurately as possible what they say. That will help you get into their world and out of your own. As you do that, you'll start to notice patterns in what they bring. That will help you answer the next step: what they need.

Some questions to help you begin to look more deeply into their needs:

- What are they avoiding?

- What is missing from what they say they want?

- What do they assume is impossible or assume is guaranteed to happen when they start moving toward what they want?

- What breakdown are they trying to avoid in their strategies?

What do they need?

Here you list the things you believe would serve your client, even if they can't see them. It's your chance to hone your coach intuition and identify opportunities to tell your clients things everyone else in their life is afraid to tell them. If you were going to design an epic fairytale that gave them everything they wanted, removed all their suffering, and surpassed all of their wildest dreams, what would you give them?

What is their soul crying out for, just hoping that someone will hear?

Most importantly, never forget that this list is something to hold very lightly. Always remember, you aren't right. This is simply what you see from your perspective.

If you cling to these things as truth, you'll soon find yourself attached to your clients following the path you've chosen for them. That isn't your job.

That said, the more you're able to spot new doorways for your clients to step into, the more you can be an invitation to walk through those doors. What you spot here will also be a reflection of what you see for yourself. (Your journey is their journey.)

Being able to spot opportunities here will give you more access to possibility in all parts of your life.

What's their breakthrough?

Your client's breakthrough opportunity is their keystone. It's the thing that, when shifted, allows every other thing they want to become more readily available. It's a complete shift in reality, a new perspective on space and time, a brand-new context.

Before a breakthrough, life looks and feels one way. They believe certain things are possible and have set rules dictating why so. After a breakthrough, life looks and feels a different way. They possess a whole host of new possibilities and rules that allow for more to exist in their world — more love, more abundance, more impact, whatever they choose.

Breakthroughs are often based on high-level themes in our lives (think money, time, trust, etc.). They encompass a full category of things rather than something specific. We don't have a breakthrough in how we communicate with our boss, for example. We have a breakthrough in relationships or intimacy everywhere in our life, and it shows up in how we communicate with our boss.

Use fear as your compass. Potential breakthroughs often lie in the things our clients are most afraid to change or let go of. Those places also happen to be where there is the most possibility and upside if they're transformed. Our clients' clinging to their current context keeps them safe, keeps them stuck, and also limits their growth if nothing shifts. Spot the source of their fear and you've spotted a world-changing breakthrough.

47

What's my breakthrough?

Imagine the Universe brought you and your client together for a reason. Not only so you could help them create in their life, but so they could help you create something new in yours (beyond just paying you money).

What might that be?
What lesson might be here for you to learn?

Don't worry, if you're like me, you might resist this part. I can find it tough to acknowledge my humanity as a coach. I'd like to not have any breakthrough opportunities and instead get everything right all the time with my clients.

Thankfully, I am a human and I do get to grow with every new client because, as I've come to learn, that helps my clients navigate their own breakthroughs. I find that acknowledging that my clients are doing a service to me helps me relate to them with gratitude and reverence. From that place, we really can create impossible things together.

Spot your breakthrough opportunities by looking at the parts of your client that get you hooked:

- What do you want to change about them?

- Where might you start pushing your own agenda?

- What's new about this engagement?

- What feelings come up when you think about this client?

- What are your growth edges right now and why did this person show up just as you were working on them?

There is no way to get any of these questions wrong. The process isn't about doing this perfectly; it's about getting in touch with your deep knowing and creating from that part of you. Test them out and adjust them as you see fit to keep on your growth path.

An example

Here are sample notes from a fictional client profile you might relate to. The client is a high-performing entrepreneur. They are highly productive, work long hours, and lead a growing team. They don't have much time for their family and don't take much time for self-care. They were referred to you because they heard coaching can be helpful as their business hits the next stage and they want to be ready.

Wants

- Be more efficient with their work, have a cleaner inbox

- To get out of the weeds of their business and think more strategically, their eye on the big picture

- Better and more consistent diet, eating on a more consistent schedule and healthier food

- Be less reactive and more present at home and work, not always checking their phone or thinking about what they have to do

I notice that just reading this list has my chest feel a little tight and my breathing restricted. I notice all of this is about getting more done.

I also notice what I imagine is a number of competing priorities in this list, which I imagine might have a feeling of overwhelm attached. All of this noticing will inform my guess about what they need but can't quite say yet.

Needs

- Rest and play. *A new context around productivity?*

- To delegate and coach team members so they can become top performers. *A new context around leadership?*

- Nervous system regulation and technology-free space

- A clear vision for the totality of life, including outcomes to focus on with diet, self-care, and family

- Acknowledgment and gratitude both inward and outward, specifically learning to receive

I notice that some of these are my own needs I'm working through. That helps me see where I might be hooked and want to push the client in a certain direction. It's helpful to shed light on that so I can look out for it.

I notice that my nervous system feels more relaxed as I write these out. There is some nervousness the client might have resistance to these which tells me I'm on the right track, and I feel solid about what I've noted.

Their breakthrough

- Trust
- Connection
- Joy/play

These are high-level themes based on the needs and wants I noted earlier. I don't want to get too detailed at this point since I'm acting in a bubble.

Instead, I want to lay the foundation from which the client can create their path and will use these to support the client in identifying what they're really working on. The wants are great and the breakthrough is what completely redefines their world.

My breakthrough

- Trust: Let the client do the work. Remain open to the magic that everyone brings to the world (including the client's family and employees who may be allies in the process). Also trust that the timing is always perfect.

- Presence + wisdom: There is nothing to do; I am a transformative presence.

These happen to be breakthroughs I'm already working on. I notice this particular client could activate my pattern of trying to be smart, trying to move them somewhere, and clinging to the path forward that I see. Perfect!

Our work together is a tremendous opportunity for me to dance with those patterns; the more adept I become at that, the more my client will also be able to realize their breakthrough in similar areas. The more I can live from trust, presence, and wisdom, the more I can allow possibility into my life. We both win.

Use these as a filter

Remember, your client isn't the only one making a yes or no decision about working together. You decide if a client is the right client for you.

Not everyone will be, for any number of reasons. As you come into your own as a coach and get clear on the work you're up to doing, you'll begin to have better discernment about who's a good fit and who isn't.

Use these questions as a filter. Feel whether their wants and needs are things you're excited to be working on. Get clear on what your breakthrough might be. If there truly is nothing there for you, this client might not be for you right now. That's okay.

Who would be the perfect coach for them right now? It's of much greater service to your client to help them find a 10/10 partnership than working with them if they aren't a good fit for you. Make the connection. It will change the world.

PART TWO:

WHAT DO

YOU WANT?

COACHING IS GPS NAVIGATION
PART TWO: BECOMING THEIR OWN GPS

WHEN I WAS in college, I lived in Madrid, Spain for six months. It was before smartphones, when I didn't have an on-demand account of where I was in the city. If I wanted to go somewhere new, I looked at a paper map and stumbled my way along based on cross streets and visual memory. There were no Yelp reviews to help me find the best places to try, either. Aside from my printed travel books or recommendations from friends, I primarily selected places based on emotions — how they looked and felt, my intuition, or some other novel reason. Pizza cones sounded cool, for example, so I decided I needed to try them. (They were so-so.) If some corner bar had a good vibe, I'd stop in, and the bar that was always empty was a place to avoid.

By the end of my time there, I knew the city quite well, almost intuitively. I could find my way around any neighborhood I'd spent time in, not always in the most direct route, but eventually. And while I didn't love every place I stopped in, I developed a great sense of what felt right for me and what didn't.

A couple of years ago, I went back to Madrid and found my way to one of my favorite spots simply by feel. I couldn't tell you the street names, but I can take you there, even if the path includes one or two extra turns.

Today, things look quite different whenever I'm out exploring. I pop some details into my phone's GPS and it tells me where to go. Or I spend 10 minutes looking at ratings before choosing which restaurant to go to. My ability to navigate the city in which I live is nothing compared to my Madrid days.

Your client is like present-day me. They've been relying on *something else* as their navigation — external sources, expectations, old patterns, trauma — accepting its directions and following every step. Even more, in many cases, that external source selects the destination for them. They've come to you because they want something their current system can't give them — something bigger, different, new, more in line with their true self, or a fuller expression of themselves.

The trouble is their current system is extremely reliable. They rarely get lost, even if the route and final destination are uninspiring. And they never take a misstep. So, giving it up is scary.

Your client is likely to try to make you their new external source for destinations and navigation. You're a brighter, shinier version of the current pattern. If you're inspiring (which you are), the destinations and directions you offer provide the promise of the bigger and different version of life they're looking for. That's a pitfall to look for.

Your job isn't to replace their GPS. *You're supporting them in becoming their own.*

Working with you helps them learn to give up external sources and become their own navigator. This includes them taking all the wrong turns, missteps, and dirt roads along the way. It also includes them learning to navigate by heart and, as you'll see in Part four, turn their car into a helicopter, submarine, or spaceship when needed.

WE'RE ALWAYS MOVING SOMEWHERE

What isn't immediately evident in my simple GPS navigation analogy is that even when we don't have the map open or directions handy, we're moving somewhere. Our location on the map is always changing, even if we don't have any destination in mind. The reality of life is that of constant change, transition, movement, and flow. Even when we're sitting still. We are always headed in some direction based on our beliefs, actions, and habits. It's like we're on a boat we captain (we'll pause the car analogy for now).

At times, we're consciously navigating the waves of life. Other times, we're asleep at the wheel. Either way, we are always in motion and always moved by life. The choice of whether we're consciously navigating the ship is ours alone. This can be a tough pill to swallow. Yet, it offers us the opportunity to become responsible for the direction we're moving and the destination we're headed toward.

And we tend to make that truth a huge thing, full of pressure and meaning about us. It's some version of the old story that says we need to get it right. It's a very human thing to do. And it isn't the only option.

WHERE DOES YOUR CLIENT WANT TO GO?

That's where we start our journey. It might feel to them like they're going from stagnant and motionless to running full speed. But remember, they're already headed somewhere. That feeling is less about the effort of beginning and more about overcoming the inertia of their current path. They're about to enter uncharted waters. Congratulations to them and to you. This is where the fun starts.

Let's find out what's next.

ON DISCOVERING WHAT WE WANT

What do you want?

It's a radical question. I imagine revolutions born thanks to someone having the courage to ask it. Once someone really digs into this question, nothing is ever the same:

- What do you want?

- What do you *really* want?

- If you could have anything at all, what would you ask for?

- What would you like?

- What dream would you dream if anything were possible?

Pause with me for just a moment and reflect on the sheer power of those inquiries. Notice what happens in your mind and body as you ask them to yourself. What are you present to? What images arise? What body sensations come alive?

For me, it's often a combination of excitement and fear. It's the joy of bringing something new into the world and receiving something that feels good. It's also the trepidation of thinking it might not happen or being shut down for what I say.

Depending on the moment, it might also be complete numbness. A blankness in my brain. The feeling of being separated from everything. It's quite a lot to be with.

Think about the questions now in comparison to how many of us were raised. What I really wanted wasn't always a consideration when I grew up. I operated mostly based on what I might be able to get. I settled, navigated in familiar waters, and lived with a constant sense that something was just a little off. It was! There were parts of me that never had a chance to speak up. They saw that more was possible for me and the world, but because their ideas didn't fit into my narrow scope, I didn't listen to them.

It's taken years to make room for more of what I truly want to come to the surface. And the bigger game I play, the more I discover things I've never seen before.

What do I want? I want to keep discovering more, letting it out, gaining strength and courage in speaking it.

What do you want?

What does your client want?

YOUR CLIENT MIGHT NOT KNOW

I don't think I'm the only one hit with that blank, numb feeling. Just the other day, I was talking with someone about coaching, and they asked what I do if someone doesn't know what they want. Aren't we all afraid of that? Don't we all experience that at some point? Not only the not knowing but the fear and judgment that come along with it? *Am I doing it wrong?*

Your client might not know what they want. They might also have a few stories about themselves because they don't. They may tell themselves that something is wrong with them, that something isn't normal, or that they're wasting your time.

Great! (I know it might not feel great for them in the moment, but that doesn't mean it's a problem.) You've established that they want to *discover* what they want. That in itself means they know what they want. That's progress. And it barely took any time.

Now, onto that discovery.

IT ISN'T ABOUT THE ANSWER

What your client says in response to the question isn't what's important. They might want ice cream today or a pink stuffed elephant or $1,000,000,000. It's about flexing a new muscle, shifting perspective, and living from a new place.

You're their trainer. When they're with you, they get to practice holding themselves to a new standard. And this standard says, "No more settling. No more accepting what's given without question. No more living small and hiding my truth. Starting now, I'm looking inside and creating from there."

You're creating the space for them to put in the reps — ugly, slow, painful, confusing, consistent reps.

This question is about shifting a context and living in a new world. You're helping your client move into an entirely new context for their life: from a recipient of others' desires and directions to the source of their own navigation.

You're reminding them of who they are: a wise, divine being connected to limitless untapped power and potential.

WE NEED SOMETHING TO PUSH AGAINST

A few years ago, I had surgery to repair my Achilles. I couldn't put weight on my leg for a couple of weeks while my foot was in a cast. The entire bottom of my leg — the calf, ankle, and foot — had no stimulation the entire time. When the doctor removed my cast, my calf was the size of my wrist and my leg felt like Jell-O. I couldn't believe how small and weak it had become in a span of just a couple of weeks. I remember getting home and spontaneously bursting into tears over the shock of it all, along with a loving desire to build my body back to health.

This is the nature of how we humans work. We don't grow in space. If anything, we shrink. It's true not only for our bodies but our minds and spirits as well. Challenges propel us forward, grant us new skills and perspectives, strengthen our resiliency, and form us into the person we envision ourselves to be.

Asking your client what they want or where they want to go isn't about them selecting the right thing. It's about them selecting their next challenge, the next mountain to climb. Any mountain. It doesn't matter. Practice is the key.

Your conversations are the training grounds for them to identify and go after new challenges everywhere in their life. Remember, they're always moving somewhere. Without a target, they're floating in space. They chose you as their coach because they want something different. They want to grow.

HOLD THE LINE

This part can get scary. For your client. For you. They'll have a whole host of things they believe are in their way of speaking what they want. (Some of them are below.)

Love them. Love them enough to stick with them and continue to invite the question.

As my coach always tells me, it's just fear. That's it. It's bound to show up whenever possibility does. Like an annoying twin sister, it hogs attention and prattles on constantly.

This is the process. They've got this. You've got this.

WHY WE DON'T KNOW WHAT WE WANT

Expect these obstacles to come up. Welcome them and see them for what they are: false evidence appearing real. They're probably quite real to your client. That's okay.

This list is written to you. See and love yourself in it first. Then see and love your clients in it. Show them the list. Invite them to identify their own stories in it. And then invite them to ask themselves what they want even with these in the way. They can still see possibility in the face of fear. That's why they're here with you.

You don't know what you want because you have either been taught or decided:

- Not to ask for what you want

63

- That what you want is too much (and therefore, you're too much)

- To just be happy with what you have

- Not to dream too big because it might not happen

- It's better to keep expectations low than to risk disappointment

- It's bad to be told no

- It's safer to ignore it than to actually look at it or ask yourself about it

- There is something wrong with you if you know what you want but don't get it

- It's easier to never actually decide what you want

- Asking makes you weak

- It's hard to ask for things

- The world/universe or people don't care

- It's unfair to others if you have more than they do

- The world doesn't give you anything without hard work

- You have to do something to deserve it (and you didn't, therefore you don't)

- Other people deserve it more

- Don't trust what you think you want, in case it's not actually what you want

- You'll just be disappointed with what you get once you have it

- Experiences are more important than things
- Frivolous things/trips/desires aren't necessary
- It's only okay to want what's necessary
- Good things come to those who wait (and likely never ask)
- There are too many choices
- You always choose wrong
- You might choose wrong this one time
- In order to receive, you have to take from someone else
- We live in a world of scarcity
- Getting what you want requires sacrifice
- You're too lazy to get it
- It isn't possible
- The cards are stacked against you anyway
- Que sera sera (whatever will be, will be)
- Wanting is not in accordance with the Tao
- Wishing for things is just a game for children
- Imagining what you want is a waste of time and energy
- All the good opportunities are already taken
- The world is cruel and dangerous and full of people who will try to take whatever you get
- The government will take it anyway

- Money is the root of all evil

- People will just hurt or screw you in the end

- Asking for something from someone hurts them or puts them in a tough spot

- You're needy or burdensome if you ask for things

- You should be reasonable or realistic

- Asking for things is unreasonable

- It's risky or dangerous to even think about, let alone ask for

- People will think you're silly/stupid/weird/[insert shit word here]

- You'll change if or once you get it

- You'll have to change in order to get it

- There is a limit to how much one person should ask for or receive

- One day, the other shoe will drop

- It's better to keep your head down than to stand out

- You'll end up alone if you get what you want

- People will be jealous or angry

- You'll lose what you already have

- Having more things means also having more things to worry about ("Mo Money Mo Problems")

- Nice things are for "other" people

- It's rude to take more than you need

- The meek shall inherit the Earth
- Try to figure out what you think you can get and ask for that
- There is significance to what you want, or to anything on this list.

I deal with these same statements too, though I'm sure interpretations vary. And they might all be true. But what if they aren't? What if we could choose to accept these or not? And what if we could also choose to accept something else instead? What would you choose? What might you ask for?

IT'S NOT THEIR FAULT

Your clients might blame themselves for not knowing what they want. They might want to let it get in the way of doing any coaching work at all. They might run in circles for days, weeks, or years as they come to learn of their own power. It isn't their fault that they don't know who they are, that they forgot they're a magical being of cosmic power. They had a multitude of factors working against them, starting before they were born on this planet. It all happened as their personality was being formed, as their brain was being developed, and before they knew what coaches even do.

Invite them to drop the blame. There is nothing and no one to fault. Everyone was trying their best and things happened as they were going to happen. We've all inherited some of the stories above. That's why there are so many!

IT IS THEIR RESPONSIBILITY

You're a stand for your client living the life that's available to them. You're a window into what's possible, and you're a mirror that reflects their infinite power back to them. Invite them to live a life without history. Invite them to heal whatever is in the way of that. Invite them to create from this moment forward, not their past. Responsibility simply means "able to respond." Help your client see that they're always able to respond. They're always able to touch the part of them that knows what they want. It cannot be lost, no matter how distant or shrouded it appears.

Even when they try to convince you that they're incapable, that they don't know how, that they're a lost cause, look for their wholeness and you'll find it. Your job is to not buy into the story. Give them the gift of trust and let them grab onto it. When they're ready, they will.

IT'S IN THERE
INVITE THEM TO FIND IT

Imagine for a moment that each of us has a universal truth running through us, like a little stream flowing through our body and mind. It's quiet, especially compared to the noise of the outside world and our constant thinking. But no matter how quiet it is, we can always feel it.

Your client wants you to help them get in greater touch with that stream of truth. They want to hear their divine intuition. They know it has something for them, something that will change their life.

Early in life, they probably put up a series of barriers to keep from hearing their truth. The barriers were meant to keep them safe — and they did — but the cost was their ability to access this divine flow.

Now they might be tempted to throw away everything they've done and do the opposite, to fight who they've been in hopes that it will lead them to who they really are. Fighting doesn't lead to peace, however. Destruction for its own sake won't get them to where they want to be. We don't discover our quiet, divine voice by cutting out the parts we don't like. It isn't by abandoning our shadows and fighting against our patterns that we find our truest expression.

We become more of ourselves by actually becoming more of our *selves*. We open the door and let them all in. You are a guest house, and your client is becoming one, as well. Help them see the holiness in every part of them, the perfection in their current self, and the beauty in their patterns. As you do, what they want will emerge. The sounds of their stream of truth will get louder and stronger. Soon, it'll be a raging river inside of them, shouting their truth on loudspeakers.

Be a source of integration and the truth will come out.

Tool: Questions that can change everything

Clients tend to put a lot of meaning and significance into what they say they want, don't they? (Don't you? I do.) It's like we stake our entire lives on the answer and accompanying result. We aren't okay right now and, if we don't get what we say we want, we'll never be okay.

Here are some of my favorite questions to help clients — and myself — move out of that stuck context and into something more fun, generative, and empowered:

- What are you committed to?

- What are you afraid to say because you think it's impossible?

- The follow-up: What are you present to now that you've said it?

- What's your diva desire?

- What would you like?

What are you committed to?

This is a question about what we stand for in our lives and the world. It invites us to view what we want as a place to come from rather than a place to get to. From that shifted perspective, I find my clients speak way more from their souls and hearts, and less from fear.

It's an invitation to look inward more deeply. Your clients might ask themselves *how* they know what they're committed to. They might start to see how their decisions have been out of alignment with their commitments, then quickly identify the patterns that get in the way.

For example, they might be committed to integrity but have a habit of lying to their partner about what they do on the weekends because they're afraid of hurt feelings. Once they see clearly that their commitment is integrity, they can get honest about what choices they now want to make to stick to that commitment (or to change their commitment).

My clients tend to be idealists, seeking big change and wanting to make the world a better place. So, this question is a powerful tool for their development as leaders.

Once in alignment with their commitments, they move through the world with force. Out of alignment, they're like a car with a broken transmission, stuttering and stopping, barely moving anywhere.

What are you afraid to say because you think it's impossible?

I have a guess that at some point in your client's life they were told something they wanted couldn't happen. It likely happened more than once or twice. And it very likely resulted in them not asking for things they thought they couldn't get. There is a part of them that's just waiting for permission to speak up without being dismissed, ridiculed, or shut down. Invite every part to the conversation and let their voices be heard.

You might be the first person in your client's life who smiles and encourages their impossible ask. By simply letting that happen, you're a source of healing. And as they practice it more and more, they'll hear more and more clearly what their true desires really are.

Remember, you're already creating the impossible. You might as well invite it to happen up front and get on board.

The follow-up: What are you present to now that you've said it?

This is where we test to see how impossible their desire is in their eyes. More impossible usually comes with more energy and excitement, maybe wonder. It also usually comes with more feelings of fear and doubt.

That's all perfect. Not because we want our clients to suffer, but because it reveals they're starting to push beyond their current boundaries and limitations. Of course, this isn't foolproof, and we don't want to push our clients toward fear indiscriminately.

Use this question to get to know your client's world. Whatever pattern emerges when they speak something huge will also likely emerge as they make progress toward making it a reality.

My partner swings from moments of extreme excitement and creativity to moments of extreme doubt and opposition when she's creating a new reality for herself. As we've gotten better at spotting this pattern, we've been able to navigate the swings with more grace and love.

Get curious with your client about what happens when they're faced with the impossible. It'll be gold now and in the future.

What's your diva desire?

This is a question I borrowed from my friend Kevin Lawrence. Like the question above, it can reveal the ways in which your client is compromising, even on their imaginary wish list. You can get creative with it, too. Have them imagine that they're a globally-adored rockstar who gets anything they want. Even things on the hidden, secret menu are available.

If there were no limits, what would they ask for? If they couldn't be turned down, what would they like?

Play make-believe and change the laws of physics with them, then watch them open up their heart.

What would you like?

This is a subtle shift from asking plainly, "What do you want?" And this shift can change things dramatically for us.

When I'm thinking about what I would like, I have more space to feel into a simple preference. For many people, there is less significance attached to their *likes* compared to thinking about their *wants*. It also tends to shift the consideration inside to what they can control.

- "I want that guy to stop being a jerk." (Can't control that.)

- "I would like to feel safety and connection." (That, I can do something with!)

Download all of the illustrations and tools from this book at www.goldenbristle.com/bookresources

ABRACADABRA AND NAMSHUBS

Since the dawn of spoken language, we humans have known the power of our speech to create our world. Have you heard of the Himba tribe? In their language, they didn't have a word for the color blue. What does that matter, you say? Well, it meant that they couldn't differentiate between things that were blue and things that were green. They literally couldn't see blue.

But they had many more words for green than we do in English. That helped them to distinguish between shades of green that you and I probably couldn't recognize. Words are magic!

Our ancestors, in touch with the natural energies of life, took great care with these powers so as to use them for good. But over the years, our knowledge of them has faded.

Let's bring them back.

Abracadabra translated from ancient Aramaic means "I will create as has been spoken." Today, we think this word just has to do with magicians pulling rabbits out of hats or making cars disappear, but those weren't its original meanings. In ancient times, abracadabra was an incantation to ward off illnesses and ailments. It acknowledges that with our *words* we create the future. It's a power word and one for us to use with intention.

Now think about the word "spell." Do you think it's a coincidence that it has to do with both the arrangement of letters to make a word and creating something magically? I don't.

When you invite your clients to give words to their desires, you're helping them cast a magic spell on the Universe. The magic of their spoken intention ripples into the world and changes everything around it. Nothing is the same after a declaration is spoken. From that moment, the Universe begins conspiring in their favor to bring their desire to them. They just have to get in the way of it and accept it once it's there.

Namshub is a Sumerian word of similar meaning: incantations, self-fulfilling prophecies, and words with magical powers. I learned of it in Neal Stephenson's book *Snow Crash*. (It's the same book that brought us the word avatar, years before the movie with blue aliens.) The Sumerians understood that when we speak things, we create things, that our words create our world.

With what words are your clients creating their worlds? My guess is that they aren't always full of light and joy. Mine aren't. My guess is they're afraid of their unfathomable power — the ability to create their world and perception of it. I, too, feel afraid at times.

But.

What if their crazy dreams aren't crazy, and instead are the Universe nudging them to open a door and explore what's there? What if they're here to cast spells with their words, to manifest something new that hasn't existed before?

It might be scary. And it might be amazing, bountiful, exhilarating, and everything they've always wanted.

That might be why it's scary.

(The same is true for you. And for me.)

By supporting your client in speaking out what they want, you're helping them create magic in the world. That, in itself, is a transformative exchange.

You're magic.

I've said it, so now it's true.

MOVING TOWARD VS. MOVING AWAY FROM

When you first ask your client what they want, they'll likely have an easier time telling you what they don't want. We're all pros at spinning tales of the parts of our life we want to get rid of, all the while holding onto them because they're familiar.

The trouble with focusing on what we don't want is that when we do that, we tend to keep it. As the saying goes:

Where attention goes, energy flows.

We move toward what we're looking at and focusing on. That's why we're taught in driving school to look at the lane ahead of us instead of the ditch on the right. Your client will be tempted to focus on the ditch. Be a loving reminder to keep their eyes on the road.

Let's say your client has been holding a 20-pound hammer and it's tiring them out. They tell you they want to stop holding the hammer, except every time they put it down, they pick it back up because that's what they're used to, and it's where their attention is taking them.

What to do?

To use another quote: Nature abhors a vacuum. Invite them to choose something to replace it with — something they want to hold that isn't a heavy hammer. Maybe it's a lollipop or a peace flag or a puppy. Now they know what they're moving toward. Now they have somewhere to place their attention and energy.

Don't get stuck on what they don't want. Invite them to give voice to what they want instead. Where there is fear, there is usually gold. Invite them to share the desires they're afraid to speak aloud.

Look for what your client believes is impossible. Look for what they avoid speaking into the world, dismiss as silly, or shut themselves down from asking for. That's the part they've long subdued and it's just waiting for a chance to have a voice.

None of those things is the right answer. You don't seek them out because scary things are good. It's because fear masks possibility. It clouds the direction of our true north and tries to obscure the way forward. When your client learns to move toward the fear rather than avoiding it, they'll get ever closer to what they truly seek.

Fear is a tool. Use it as such.

PREDICT AND MANAGE VS. DECLARE AND FULFILL

In response to being conditioned to not ask for or seek out what they truly want, your client's first attempt will likely not reflect their true desires. They'll resort to the same strategies that have gotten them exactly where they are. The following distinctions will help them move beyond that and into the life of their true dreams.

When we *predict and manage*, we ask for things in the future based on our current life trajectory. If we're making $80,000 this year, we shoot for $90,000 next year to beat inflation and have some more spending money. If we took a week-and-a-half-long vacation this year, next year we shoot for taking two separate weeklong trips. Growth is incremental rather than transformational or exponential.

Our predictions are based on being reasonable and realistic. They aim to limit disappointment, thus offering the guise of safety. They feel less risky than asking for more because they appear attainable. Often, our identity or worth is tied to reaching these goals, so we do what we can to avoid failure, even at the expense of our truth.

As a rule, any goal spoken within the context of predict-and-manage must fit entirely into our current ideas for what's possible and available to us. We then manage our lives in accordance with these predictions. Usually, this looks like balancing all the things in our life that we put at odds with each other. Spend some time over here at work, some time over here for fitness, then the rest is divvied across friends and family. We try to fit everything into its nice little box so nothing is ever upset.

The downside of this context is that nothing is ever truly great or what we actually want. We never break free from the balancing act we're doing to actually receive what life wants to offer. We slowly feel less and less alive.

A more empowered context for moving toward what we want is to declare and fulfill. A declaration requires an energetic shift away from attaching our identity to our goals and toward regarding our worth as inherent and unquestioned. We choose to declare what we want because we can (we are God, after all) and our declarations arise from our desires and commitments.

Once we're released from having our identity attached to our vision, the act of fulfilling it becomes an exploratory game. We can step back and simply ask ourselves what needs to happen to bring what we want to reality (like looking at the directions our GPS offers on the way to our next destination). We move, evaluate, and more again.

For our clients, the act of declaring from this place necessarily moves them out of their current realm of what's possible. If they're used to holding back from speaking what they actually want because it feels impossible, declaring and fulfilling requires a brand-new way of acting. It is creating something impossible. Who they have to be to accomplish it has to shift and the way in which they view the world has to shift.

That's transformation.

The more they learn to declare and fulfill in life, the more they grow into their divine power and wisdom. The world feels less at odds with them (or anyone else) and the idea of having it all is no longer crazy talk. Everything is available.

HONEST VS. REALISTIC

Raise your hand if you were taught to be realistic when you were growing up. I was. What that meant was to temper my expectations and tune down my desires based on what I thought the world might give me. I don't blame my parents or the others who instructed me in that way. That's what they learned, too, and they were doing the best they could to keep me from feeling disappointed.

The result, however, was that I stopped listening to the voice inside that knew what I wanted and, instead, started listening to the one that was always compromising. My menu of choices shrank and shrank. The world evolved into a place defined by competition instead of collaboration.

My disappointment didn't go away (I don't think it ever really does.). Rather, I lived a life wishing and hoping for things I didn't actually want but thought might be attainable. And when I didn't get those, my requests shrank even more. Or I turned the disappointment inward, telling myself that if I couldn't even get the watered-down version of things, I certainly didn't deserve anything better.

I'm willing to bet your client has been taught the same thing. Most of us have. It feels safer to set our expectations based on what others tell us is possible than to listen to our hearts and ask for something that might be impossible.

The cost is enormous, though. Our menu shrinks and shrinks while our fear of straying outside its boundaries grows and grows. Before we know it, we're left with only a handful of options every day: which clothes to wear to work, which show to watch when we get home, or where to order dinner delivery.

Our true desires are buried more every day.

Being *realistic* limits what's possible for us without actually reducing our disappointment. Don't let your client fall into the trap of realistic. Support them in being *honest*. Honestly naming what they want is a courageous act. It not only flies in the face of what your client was taught when they were young, it also introduces fear immediately.

Their honest desires might come with judgment attached, stories about failure, or what happens if they don't reach them. Or they'll come with stories about what happens if they do reach them, or the changes that success will bring to their life and relationships.

Being honest about what they want is not without its risks for your client. Their entire life is built around keeping things how they are right now. Upsetting that system will cause ripple effects neither of you can completely predict. Acknowledge the fear. Understand it. Then point to what's true: They're working with you because they want something different. That little voice of honesty wants to be heard. Your job is to support them in letting that out so they can see things as they are and know themselves in their full expression.

Invite your clients to be honest about their desires and teach them to spot when they are instead being realistic. Let that voice out. See where impossible might take them.

DESIRE VS. SHOULD

Your client has been brainwashed. They likely believe the things they've been told to want are what they actually want. And they might be. But probably not. Not exactly, at least. (It's okay to not get this right. It's okay to not get anything right, as if there was a right answer to begin with. It requires patience, courage, and quiet attunement.)

Most of the time, *should* arises from burden or imposition. It's what we believe we need to do to get something from someone else or from the world. Often, it's strategies we believe will be effective in filling a true desire or need.

- We should make money so our partner will stay with us.

- We should exercise so we can be more attractive.

- We should stay in our corporate job so our parents will approve of our decisions.

The more we dig into shoulds, the more we can spot what's underneath them:

- The need to feel loved

- The need for connection and safety

- The desire for an intimate romantic relationship

- The desire to be a provider

There is nothing inherently wrong with shoulds, they just aren't the real thing. And our clients are opening themselves in our work so they can touch the real thing. I find them to be quite informative in moving toward true *desire*:

- "I should have known" reveals a desire to be wise or discerning. It says that, in the future, I'd like to make a better decision.

- "This shouldn't be so hard" reveals that I want something to be easy. And it reveals that I find it hard at the moment.

- "I should be better at this by now" reveals something similar. It says that I want to feel good at what I'm doing and get better results.

These statements also reveal an unmet (unreasonable) expectation: that life will be different from how it is currently or was in the past. Of course, life can't be different, or else it would be. What we get right now is what we get. Only in the future can it change.

SHOULDING ALL OVER OURSELVES

So, if the *should* isn't the issue, what is? It's our relationship to the should. It's the meaning, significance, and power we give it. A should directed toward ourselves becomes a sort of dagger, piercing straight into our self-concept. We poison it with the message of "I'm not good enough," "I'm not worth loving," or something similar. And, often, these messages go unseen by our conscious mind as they damage our unconscious view of ourselves.

When we direct these statements **outward**, toward others or toward the world, it's us spreading the poison we've cultivated within. We share our own **fears** and inadequacies, hoping that someone else will pick **them** up and share the load.

What this creates is a disempowering relationship with the world and ourselves: "I'm not good **enough** and the world isn't any better."

I feel the impact of that statement as I write it. It's a feeling of defeat and sadness.

The upside is that we can change our relationship to should if we want and choose to:

- We can learn to catch ourselves when we say it and notice where we are adding significance, and what emotion it evokes.

- Then we can ask ourselves what desire the should reveals.

- Finally, we can ask if and how we'd like to commit to creating that desire in the world.

As an example, we'll use the statement: "I should be making more money by now."

- **Significance/meaning**: I'm not good enough. I'm not living up to my potential and am a bad business owner. I'm letting people down.

- **Emotion**: Sadness, fear, shame.

- **Desire**: I'd like to create more money in my life, starting this month. I'd like to have a feeling of belonging and connection with others. I'd like safety.

- **Action**: I'm going to enroll a new client in the next 30 days, or I'm going to schedule a meeting with my boss to ask for a raise.

- **Alternative action**: No, I don't need to take action right now. I'm actually quite happy with how much money I make, and those stories about not being enough aren't true. Instead, I will choose to say something true and kind to myself when I notice this fear coming up. I'm going to call a friend and share my desire for connection and safety.

As we honor the emotions present and look underneath them at what's really going on, we have the space to reveal a true desire and choose the right action for us.

DRAWING OUT DESIRE

Our desires arise from within. We might not know the source, but we know they feel true. There is a purity to them. They're free from the "so that..." or "once I..." that attach themselves to shoulds.

Desires open new possibilities. We might ask, "Am I allowed to ask for that?" We might have a sheepish smile after naming a desire. They often feel tender.

And with possibility, they bring fear. They might feel scary to touch, especially when they fall into the context of our identity or worth.

We'll say, "Someone like me doesn't ask for something like that." That's how we know we're on the right track.

Desires aren't always meant to come true. They might be stepping stones to something else. We don't name them so they become ours to hold onto. We name them so that we get better at naming them, better at hearing our souls speak.

Invite your client to get quiet and listen to the whispers of their desires, even if they sound crazy or unfounded. Give light to what they've long buried. Call forward the music of their soul.

Tool: Goals, experience, and What For

When you invite your client to envision where they want to go, invite them to consider three different aspects of that vision:

- Goals: The tangible and specific outcomes your client wants in life.

- Experience: How they want it to go along the way, and how they want to feel while they're working toward or once they realize their goal.

- What For: The bigger reason for this goal in their life, and what becomes possible on the other side of realizing both the objective and experience of it.

Goals: What are the outcomes you'd like?

Goals are the tangible outcomes your clients want in life. They're the trips they want to take, the money they want to receive, the home they want to enjoy, and the marathon in which they want to compete.

Goals and outcomes are often specific, measurable, and time-based to be most effective. The clearer your clients get about the parameters of their goals, the better they're able to determine if they're on track or off track.

Examples:

- I want to have a salary of $250,000 this year.

- I want to take two weeks of vacation and sail between Caribbean islands.

- I want a four-bedroom house in Seattle with a grass yard for my puppy.

- I want to perform during the Super Bowl halftime show.

When people first start to imagine what they want, tangible things like money, achievements, or other successes are usually the first things that come to mind. That's okay and it's a great place to start. Too many times, though, clients will end there without examining any further. When that happens, they miss out on the reasons they want those things in the first place.

Experience: How do you want things to go?

Invite your clients to step beyond just the tangible aspect of their desire and into the feeling of it. How do they want it to feel as they climb their mountain? What relationship do they want with the journey itself, or with reaching the summit? How do they want to feel about themselves along the way? What impacts will this target have on other parts of their life (if they could have it all)?

Examples:

- I want to feel excited about the work I'm doing and lovingly maintain the work/life boundaries I've set up recently.

- I want the planning process to be fun and restful.

- I want to be in partnership with my Realtor® and remain open to ideas that aren't my own.

- I want to surrender to the moment and trust the work I've done to get here.

Your client might tend to focus entirely on the experience they want to have of life. They want to feel peace or confidence in their work, for example. Or they want better friendships or deeper relationships. From this place, they might forego naming specific outcomes because they fear having such goals will prevent them from having the experience they want. They'll decide they just want to go with the flow of life and not be attached to a goal. Or when a goal gets challenging, they'll drop it because it doesn't feel in alignment.

This pattern is pointing to a context of either/or and if/then, based on being attached or resigned to achieving goals.

Spotting If/Then and Either/Or

Look out for your clients believing that achieving one of their outcomes will cause them to feel a certain way (or vice versa):

- They want to have $1 million in the bank so they can feel at peace about their finances.

- They want to get a new job title so they can feel successful and happy with their career choice.

- They want to feel confident so they can meet a potential romantic partner.

- Or they want to be able to trust their friends more so they can share more openly with them.

Thought about this way, life (and moving toward what they want) is a series of if/then statements:

- "If this happens, then I can feel something positive."

- "Once I feel positive, then I will take action."

This is a cue for you as a coach to get curious about your client's world. Notice where they've put unconscious limitations on themselves and the world as they start to ask themselves about the experience of life they want. For example, maybe they'd like to double their income but believe it's impossible to do while also having an experience of time freedom. Or they want to start a family but believe they'll have to give up freedom and travel.

What if you could have both?

By inviting your client to create both the tangible outcomes and the experience of life they desire at the same time, you can invite the possibility of something beyond either/or.

What if both were possible?

What if both and even more were available? What if having both opened up more fun, joy, success, or flourishing in their life? Then, how might it look to begin to create that?

They can have it all... if they want it.

What For: What is the purpose?

Underneath your client's desires lies something more potent. It's the fuel that will drive them when everything feels like an uphill battle and they've forgotten why they turned onto this road in the first place. It's their What For. Call it their Why if you'd like. Their What For is the change they seek to create in the world, connected to their larger purpose, their North Star. (They all deserve capital letters because they're important for your client.) It's why they get up and do what they do. It's the crazy dream they believe is possible for them, their children, and the world as everyone begins to transform. This vision might be difficult to touch at first, but once uncovered it will want to bring itself into the light.

You want to identify your client's What For upfront because fear loves to obscure it in the middle of a journey. Fear thrives in the absence of clarity, and nothing provides greater clarity than a driving purpose.

Invite your client to write their What For down and have it everywhere they look. Encourage them to come back to it daily. Tattoo it on their arm and print t-shirts with it displayed — whatever they can do to return here early and often.

When they keep their What For in mind, nothing can stop them.

Examples

Goals: The tangible and specific outcomes your client wants in life.

Examples:

- I want to have a salary of $250,000 this year.

- I want to take two weeks of vacation and sail between Caribbean islands.

- I want a four-bedroom house in Seattle with a grass yard for my puppy.

- I want to perform during the Super Bowl halftime show.

Experience: How they want it to go along the way.

Examples:

- I want to feel excited about the work I'm doing and lovingly maintain the work/life boundaries I've set up recently.

- I want the planning process to be fun and restful.

- I want to be in partnership with my realtor and remain open to ideas that aren't my own.

- I want to surrender to the moment and trust the work I've done to get here.

What For: The bigger reason for this goal in their life, and what becomes possible on the other side of realizing both the objective and experience of it.

Examples:

- I'm committed to both securing my family's financial future and doing work I care about. With this goal realized, I'll be open to a whole new realm of money, generosity, and abundance in life. From there, I'll be able to try out new projects that I've held back from.

- Adventure is something I value and a priority going forward. I'll redefine my relationship with time off and tap into my sense of exploration.

- This is about more than a new house, it's about relationships. When I make this happen with my Realtor®, I'll know I can co-create with others in a brand-new way and learn to receive more from others.

- Performing for me is about expression. On the world's biggest stage, I'll know I can create new forms of art by trusting myself. Afterwards, have an even larger platform to use to inspire others to express themselves.

Download all of the illustrations and tools from this book at www.goldenbristle.com/bookresources

WHAT GAME ARE YOU PLAYING?

We're all playing multiple games in our lives, all the time. We're doing things because we think they'll help us win and get the prize each week. You're playing several games: the coach game, the friend game, the son/brother/daughter/sister/cousin game. Your clients are playing games too. The games we play run our lives. And most of them are unconscious. We play the same games we learned as kids, with the same rules and strategies, challenges, and objectives. Most often, they're games our parents passed down to us. They might not have even known they were playing them.

Your client is winning every one of the games they're playing, but they might not actually be playing for the outcome they think they are:

- They might think they're playing to spend more time with their family but, instead, they're playing to maintain their identity as someone whose value is derived from working hard.

- They might think they're playing the game of growing deep, intimate relationships with friends but, instead, they're playing to prove true their family's belief that other people cannot be trusted.

They work with you to reveal the games they're playing so they can choose new ones if they'd like.

WHAT GAME DO YOU ACTUALLY WANT TO PLAY?

Your client is a game master. Invite them to design a game they'd love to play and win.

- What if they could make up the rules any way they wanted, choose to win every day, and always select a strategy that delighted them?

- What if things didn't have to be so serious and they could simply play and have fun because they choose to?

- And what if winning or losing didn't have to mean anything about their worth as a person?

They're likely making things more complicated than they need to be. Challenge them to discover what they're really playing for and see where things go from there.

IT FEELS LIKE A WASTE OF TIME

This is all going too slowly, Matt. My client wants results. They want to take action and blast through their limitations. That's why they hired me. That's what feels good to them and to me.

I get it. We're accustomed to believing that progress and action are the only measures of success. And I'm not telling you to not coach or move forward. If you're still here, however, my guess is that something is still missing for you and your client. They still aren't crystal clear on what success would look like and how to measure it.

> *I don't think you do get it. Focusing so much on what they want is annoying them. What if they want to quit?*

What if they want to quit on getting more clear than they've ever been about the life they want, pulling it closer to themselves the whole time, learning to act as if it's *already here*?

That sounds perfectly human and natural. And I wonder how often and where that bias toward quitting shows up in their life. I wonder what it's like for them to be in the discomfort of trusting themselves to ask for what they want.

I wonder what it's like for you to be in that discomfort, too. How does this go for you?

IT'S OKAY TO SPEND THE WHOLE TIME HERE

Imagine you are your client. You've checked all the boxes over the years in your life. You've followed the path laid out. People around you would say that you're quite successful, but you know something is missing. Now, for the first time in your life, someone is asking you what you actually want. They aren't forcing. They aren't interrupting or correcting. They aren't ridiculing or belittling. If anything, they're encouraging. The more you talk, the more they slow down and listen. It's like you're their whole world right now.

A new part of you is opening up. It's a part that you've feared revealing for a long time because it never got this kind of attention before. It feels quite funny, uncomfortable even. But you like it, too. And that seems weird. This person is inviting you to ask for things you didn't even know were allowed. You're looking at parts of your life you'd given up on changing. That's the discomfort. What if you start dreaming, then nothing changes?

Still, they don't seem to need anything from you (unlike pretty much everyone else in your life). They won't leave or judge you if you don't make these new dreams happen. Their demands are different: that you get to what's real for you, that you be honest with yourself, even if nothing changes.

Wait. They'll love you even if nothing changes like you say it will? And they'll love you if everything does change, too?

You realize you might as well go for the gold. What do you really want? What if you made this question a practice every day? What might shift?

THIS PART ISN'T EXTRA IT'S PART OF THE JOURNEY

Really, there is no extra. Everything is part of the journey. For a professional athlete, game day starts the day before, if not sooner. It's visible in what they eat, when they go to bed, how they prepare their mental state, and what they spend their time on until the minute the game starts. Nothing is separate.

The same is true for your client and the journey they're on. Everything leading up to now was a part of the journey and everything after will be, as well. Every moment you two have spent together is a part. The agreements and container you created together (or are creating now) are a part. They all add up and they all fit together to move your client forward.

Putting meticulous attention on each step is a way to honor the role each one plays.

YOU ONLY THINK THERE IS SOMEWHERE TO GET TO

Where are you rushing to? The coaching part? The end, when everything is wrapped up in a bow? How do you know when that will be? Do they know? What are you missing by looking ahead?

Take a breath. Touch this moment. It's the only one that really exists.

What's happening right now for your client? For you?

WHAT THEY WANT VS. WHAT YOU WANT

You aren't always going to agree with your client. In fact, I think it's better if you don't because it means you're working with people who challenge your assumptions and beliefs about the world.

They won't think like you think. They won't want what you want.

Your work is to let go of what you want in service of what they want. In order to do that, it's helpful if they're crystal clear on what exactly they want. That gives less room for your brilliant ego to step in and assume for them. It's that assumption that leads to coaching conversations to nowhere.

The tricky part is that you're also watching out for your client's survival mechanisms deciding what they want. If you're supporting them in creating something new, their old patterns are pretty much guaranteed to show up and try to drive the bus. So how, then, do coaches support clients in what they want when you'll both do things to try to sabotage it? You practice remaining a stand for your coaching being about what your client wants. You mess up. You lean too far to one side, then back to the other. You acknowledge that it's a part of being human. All the while, you strengthen your muscles in coming back to your client.

There is no exact formula to help you distinguish between when you are choosing what your client wants instead of allowing them to make this choice. That, I believe, is the beauty of this work. There are, however, some things to look out for, and some tools to use.

1. **Notice who's doing most of the work.** Does it feel like you're pulling your client out of the hole over and over again? Are you asking questions to try to get them somewhere?

2. **Notice when you need them to get somewhere.** Telltale thoughts are the same as when we're hooked (because you are hooked if you want to change your client's mind):

   o   If they just...

   o   I really wish they'd...

- ○ They need to see this...

- ○ How can I get them to...?

3. **Check in with them**. Over and over again, more often than you think you need to. Ask them how the conversation is going. Ask them if you're moving closer to what they want. Ask them if their request is still the same. If you have an interpretation of their words, ask them if it's accurate. Understand their world.

4. **Notice when you're being right**. If you believe your client is coming from fear or a survival mechanism, great. Offer the observation. But don't be right about it. Invite them to share their perspective and be curious and open. Remember, you're supporting them to be their own navigation system, not to rely on you as The Mirror of Truth.

5. **Notice when you think you know which direction is best**. This, I believe, is the source of most circular coaching sessions. It manifests as a combination of the things above.

Coaches receive a vague request, assume they know what it means, start driving the client in one direction and never check in along the way. After an hour, they both look up and have no idea where they went. It may have felt good. There may have been an insight or cathartic release. But the client didn't get a chance to flex their direction-setting muscles.

None of this is to say that your humanity and direction are not welcome inside a coaching space. Part of our role as coaches is to provide clear, agreed-upon boundaries for our

101

clients. If, for example, a new topic arises toward the end of a session, our job might be to guide the client to pause on that topic in service of the time container. That's different from deciding someone needs to quit their job and "coaching" them in that direction because we've concluded it's best for them.

I'm giving excess time and attention to this topic to remind you to do the same in *your* coaching conversations. Take this level of intention into your next session and go painstakingly slow with your client in service of them speaking their desire.

It might feel uncomfortable for both of you. That's okay. Trust that you can both handle whatever comes up and look for the gold that emerges. I promise, there will be plenty.

RINSE AND REPEAT (PART ONE)

Your client's mind is like a puppy in training. And it's not just their mind either. It's your mind and my mind and all of our minds. When you take a puppy out for a walk, it goes everywhere. Everything is interesting. It doesn't follow commands, pulls on the leash, eats whatever it can, and seeks the new at every opportunity.

Eventually, the puppy can start to gain discipline. It can learn to walk in a straight line while ignoring the squirrel running up a nearby tree. It will pull less on the leash and, instead, move in a consistent direction. It simply takes patience and consistency on your part when doing the training.

When it comes to remaining clear on what we want so we can move in that direction, patience and consistency are the key ingredients there as well. As your client moves from being able to visualize their desire in their mind to articulating it to others, then to believing and embodying ownership of the desire, each step requires repetition.

Remember, most of us don't have **much** practice asking for what we want. And your job as a **coach** is to support your client in becoming their own navigation system in pursuit of that. Help them to put in the reps.

- On each call, are they clear about what they're playing for, or what their big **vision** is?

- Are they clear on where they **want** to go during your time together?

- At any given moment in the **conversation**, can they identify what they want next?

- In between your sessions, are **they** being reminded of the reason behind the **transformation** they're creating?

You might think asking these **questions** once is enough. I assure you, it is not. Even when you **feel** bored of them, even when your clients feel frustration about coming back to them. Every repetition strengthens their muscles. Every new answer clarifies things a bit more.

1. What do you want?
2. Where are we going?
3. What's your desire in this **moment**?
4. What's all this for?
5. Rinse and repeat.

Every step is a new perspective. **What** if your client didn't have to get what they want right the **first** time? What if they had infinite chances to clarify and adjust and shift and try again? The truth is, they do. Whether or not they see it, however they feel about it, they do. They can keep going or stop or shift course at any moment.

Keep returning here. Support them by being in the practice of coming back to their commitment, touching possibility once more, and re-enrolling themselves in their own life. Not because you say so, but because they want to.

Because that's what they're choosing.

Over and over again.

Watch magic happen in real time.

They've got this. You've got them.

PART TWO: WHAT DO YOU WANT?

PART THREE:

WHERE ARE YOU

RIGHT NOW?

COACHING IS GPS NAVIGATION
PART THREE: CURRENT LOCATION

LET'S GO BACK to the days of MapQuest printed directions. We'd go to the computer, enter two locations, and get a list of instructions on how to get from one place to the other. Then we'd take our printed papers into the car and do our best to track ourselves along the way. I have friends who would even reset their trip odometers to measure how long we'd been driving on each road to assure we made the correct next move. A missed turn could cost us a ton of time if we didn't notice it quickly.

This system was helpful but imprecise compared to today's navigation systems that can pinpoint our location down to a few feet. Missed turns are caught immediately. As we turn, the orientation of the map turns with us, so we always have a clear view of what's ahead. It'll even show us a picture of the address so we can make sure we're in the right place.

Sometimes, though, my navigation system loses track of me. It thinks I'm headed south when I'm actually going north. Or it thinks I'm down the block when I order a rideshare and sends the driver to the wrong place. In those moments, my system is in breakdown. When my GPS can't locate me, any directions it offers won't help me get to where I want to go. Or if they do, they'll make me take a few extra steps that could have been avoided.

Knowing where we are at any given moment is vital in calculating the next step toward where we want to go. Without it, we're prone to turn in circles. For some clients, that critical component is missing.

I've talked with many people who have an idea of coaching — or moving toward any goal, really — that resembles a battle leader from the Middle Ages. It's the scene where our hero identifies the enemy to be conquered, raises his sword, and charges headlong at them, ignoring whatever is happening on the battlefield along the way. He doesn't look around or adjust until he's encountered the target and engaged. Meanwhile, chaos ensues in every direction. I get why we might do this, and it can be an effective way to approach some obstacles, but it certainly isn't the only way.

Let's examine an often-overlooked part of the coaching journey: where you are now. And we'll begin by taking an honest look at how we all tend to screw it up so that we can get a clearer picture of how to identify our current location more accurately.

ON BEING HERE

We spend most of our lives running away from being here, in this moment, with life as it really is. There is a multi-billion-dollar industry (meditation, yoga, coaching) being built on helping us to be here, and it's designed to combat the multi-trillion-dollar industries (social media, television, alcohol) that attempt to pull us away from being here.

I find great discomfort and great peace in the moments I'm really here. I would suspect you and your clients experience something similar. I feel sadness in reading those words as I write them. What's in that?

If we slow down long enough, I believe we spot the inherent tension of the human condition. On one hand, the divine part of us knows something else is available for us, that there is magic here for us all, right now. On the other hand, we also know we're the ones keeping ourselves from it. So we grasp and pull, push and reject. We work ourselves up in a tizzy day after day in that tension. We thrash against our true nature, all the while demanding what we don't yet have, what we say we want.

The truth about your clients? They already have what they want—at least 51 percent of them does. (If more than 50 percent of us doesn't want something, we change it.) If they wanted something different, they'd do something different. They'd be something different. Understand this first.

Their life is the perfect result of their perfect system for getting exactly this. It makes complete sense. There is nothing wrong with it. Don't let them convince you otherwise.

Don't let your own survival mechanisms convince you otherwise. There's wisdom in where they are right now.

And.

Your client is talking to you because some part of them wants something different. Honor both of those parts. They're both real, and they both have an important voice in the conversation.

It can all be true. Invite that into the space and see what shifts.

THE OBSTACLES AREN'T THE LOCATION

Your clients might disagree that they (or you) are overlooking where they are now. If they're anything like me, they will go on and on and on about how they perceive their current situation — the ways they're a victim, why it's so hard to identify or have what they want, the silly thoughts in their head, and everything else stopping them from living their best life. Look closely at most of those things. They aren't actually where your client is right now or what's really going on. They're what your client believes is in the way. And we ain't there yet, friend.

A more accurate description of where they are right now is they're in a state of describing their obstacles. They're lost in thoughts and feelings, hooked, or otherwise living in the wreckage of their future, as my coach would say.

Invite them to slow down and take a breath. Support them in getting unhooked and getting real about what's around them.

THEY'RE HOOKED

The nice thing about our trusty GPS apps is they have no agenda for us. They don't have judgments about where we are or where we're headed. They don't have feelings about how long it's taking to get somewhere or opinions on our route versus someone else's. They also don't worry about what their mom would think about the directions they give. They don't point out that the guy next to us is pulling ahead or has a nicer car. They simply report our location based on the data they have and offer their guidance in accordance.

The same is not true for your clients (or you, or any of us). Our brains generously offer all those things, all the time. We have opinions on reality compared to how we think it should be. We have stories about how things should have happened in the past, should be happening right now, and should continue to happen in the future. We have feelings about the opinions and stories that influence our behaviors.

All of these things combine to muddy the data your clients use to track their location. And they all influence the directions your clients' metaphorical GPS offers them. Caught in our human clamoring for things to be different — to be somewhere other than where they currently are — your clients have a distorted view of what's true. The road ahead of them looks blocked. They're surrounded by people trying to get in their way, stop their progress, and generally cause them harm. Or all they see are people who are better than them, moving more quickly toward an imagined destination, or blessed to not suffer the same afflictions they do. They've tried every available route, and nothing has worked.

When a person is in a place of not accepting their current situation, they're hooked. They're hooked to an alternate version of reality that doesn't exist, and to their thoughts and feelings about it.

Being hooked is just like it sounds. It's like having a giant fish hook lodged in their side, pulling in the direction of the reality they believe should exist — the one in their mind they believe will allow them to escape the discomfort of the current moment.

But instead of being a fish, your client is an immovable object. And since they can't escape their current reality (remember: immovable), all it accomplishes is more pain.

Fun, right?

YOU'RE HOOKED

- The part of your client that annoys you? Hook.

- Your desire to help them out of their current hole (the one they fall into every single week)? Hook.

- Your fear that makes you a bad coach? Your fear that your client will figure it out and fire you? Your fear that your client will get annoyed that they keep falling into the hole and fire you? Hook. Hook. Hook.

If you're doing great work, if you're supporting people as they transform their reality, if you're working with clients who inspire you and take on impossible missions, you're going to get hooked. That's just part of the job.

The good news is, we all get hooked. If you or your client are anything like me, you get hooked multiple times a day. That's okay. It's human. It's even more expected when we're navigating uncharted territory. We want things to be different from how they are. We want the past to have gone differently. We want our imagined future to go differently (even though we're creating it). We want our present to be different, even if we can't describe how.

Whenever those thoughts are coming up, we're hooked. And the more we pull, the more the hook digs in. Instead, we can use them as a signal that it's time to get real about where we really are and what's really going on. It's time to take a pause and stop pulling.

When we stop moving and start looking honestly at our current situation, we're participating in a courageous act. It's also a necessary one. The willingness to see and feel beneath the stories of blame, victimhood, and denial that we all share, at times, brings the gift of a new perspective.

Here are just a few hooks. I fall into these traps often. If we're doing good work, it's inevitable. Getting unhooked is the key:

- You want your client to like you.

- You want your client to keep paying you.

- You want your client to feel better.

- You're afraid to make a mess that you can't clean up.

- You're afraid they're in a hole they can't get out of alone.

- You think you're right.

- You believe your client's stories.

- Your identity is tied to keeping this client — the impact they're making, their job title, not getting fired so you can have a full practice and make six figures, etc.

- Your client's stuff is mixed with yours.

Feel free to add your own here so you know what to look out for.

SOME SIGNS YOUR CLIENT (OR YOU, OR ANYONE) IS HOOKED

How do you tell if you're hooked? If you aren't fully in acceptance of life right now, in this moment, you can assume that you are. There are some telltale phrases that someone who is hooked will use. Once you know them, I suspect you'll start to spot them all over the place. It's your new superpower. They are:

- "I know I need to..."
- "If they just..."
- "I wish I/they/you would have..."
- "Why can't..."
- "I/they should..."

The list goes on and on. Anger, sadness, frustration, and shame are emotions that often accompany being hooked.

If you want to spot where you get hooked, go back to Part one and dig a bit deeper into where you think your client is wrong and you're right, where their vision scares you, and where you're rushing ahead. Those are all juicy spots for coaches to get hooked.

How do you get unhooked? Well, first stop pulling so hard.

Tool: How to unhook

This tool is one for you to use first. Try it out for yourself before bringing it to your clients. As you go through the steps, notice what arises for you — what's challenging, what's obvious, and what you want to ignore or skip past. All of that is welcome. Take it slow.

Step 1: Acknowledge that you're hooked

This might be an obvious step, but it can be easy to overlook. Generally, we don't like to acknowledge that we're hooked. We'd rather be right about why our current victim perspective is justified. We'd rather continue swimming in a sea of emotions, denying what's true, and making the world at fault for our life. But there is no way to remove the hook if we don't know it's there.

Slow down. Take a breath. Put your awareness on what's actually happening. Look for the signs of being hooked and take special notice of what they look like for you. Then acknowledge that you have a hook in you somewhere.

Step 2: Stop trying to unhook

The genius design of hooks is that they anticipate something pulling against them. They're designed to hold more strongly the more oppositional force is added. (Hats off to the inventor.) That's true in the emotional world just as it is in the physical world. In order to remove a hook, we need to first stop struggling against it:

- Keep being slow.

- Relax into it.

- Notice there is less discomfort as you pull less.

- You might have a more acute awareness of the hook now. Relax into that, too. It's okay.

- Notice what arises for you as you relax. What emotions arise? What happens in your body or your mind? What parts of your identity are talking?

- Notice the imagined reality it's trying to pull you toward without running away from the current one. What are you hoping it will gain for you? What's the real need or desire underneath it?

Step 3: Lean into it

Removing the hook fully requires a movement that feels backward. It's counterintuitive to our survival mechanisms because it can feel like it's bringing us in the direction of danger. But it's the only way off the hook.

Get out a pen and write this all down. Move the energy out of your head and onto something tangible to clear the hook's charge within you:

- What are you mad, sad, resentful, ashamed, or judgmental about?

- What are you afraid of right now?

- What are you trying to eject or escape from?

- What wisdom lies in that emotion?

- What's true, right now, in this moment?

Notice what arises for you as you look directly at these things. What emotions arise now? What happens in your body or your mind?

Notice what shifts or opens. Then begin to own what's here now.

- How was everything going to line up the way it did, no matter what, to get us here?

- How are they right (without you being wrong)?

- How are you responsible (without being to blame)?

- How is this current moment perfect?
- What is here for you to feel fully?
- What's the lesson to be learned?

Step 4: Choose anew

With the hook out of your side, take a look around you once more. From this new place, connect with your vision and bring your destination to mind. Now ask, based on your commitment, what's next?

Keep breathing.

Proceed with love.

Download all of the illustrations and tools from this book at www.goldenbristle.com/bookresources.

HONEST, ACCEPTING, LOVING, ACCURATE

The key to unhooking is to begin to see things as they are versus how we want them to be or how we think they should be. It's like removing glasses that distort our view of things so we can see life as it is.

As a coach, our job is to hold this perspective for our clients, remaining as clear and true a mirror as we can be. For our clients, it means having the courage to step out of their current, clouded world and into something different.

An unclouded perspective has four main characteristics:

1. Honest
2. Accepting
3. Loving
4. Accurate

If you like acronyms, feel free to call it HALA. I never have, but you can.

Honest

We covered honest when it came to what your client wants. It's just as valuable when they're identifying where they are right now. Honest means giving room to all of what is present or emerges — the silly, the scary, the embarrassing, the funny, the exciting, the inspiring, the powerful, the dark, and the divine. It's a true account of the expansiveness in each of us.

Honest requires tremendous courage. It often dredges up the mucky feelings we've kept hidden for many years. Our perspective stops being based on what we want to see, what we hope others will see, where we'd like to be, or where we think we should be by now. It's spilling our guts even when we find it uncomfortable.

Guilt and shame often come up when we begin to get honest. True honesty is acknowledging them without becoming attached to or identifying with them (i.e., getting hooked).

Honesty isn't a trip on the blame roller coaster. It's looking those feelings in the eye and acknowledging that they're walking by.

Accepting

We could call this non-judgmental. Accepting is recognizing the stories we have about how things are supposed to be compared to how they are now. It's releasing the habit to run or to try to move somewhere else and accepting that such a habit exists in the first place. Allowing things to be exactly as they are. Relaxing control.

Accepting requires us to loosen our grip. It's a spiritual practice, acknowledging that we alone cannot control everything that happens — in our own mind and body, let alone the world around us.

Accepting invites us to receive and then embody divine grace, eventually spreading it freely and widely.

Loving

Loving is offering compassion toward ourselves and our life as a whole as we go through this process. It's seeing things could not have gone differently and recognizing we're trying our best. It involves feeling the tenderness that comes with sitting with what is.

Loving requires an open heart. It touches something deep within us: our connection to everything. It's a tremendous act of strength, especially when tears well and sadness or grief flow through us.

Love is also a powerful energizer, much more so than anger and violence. It is what softens us such that the hook can be removed fully. Only then can we move forward.

Accurate

As we practice honesty, acceptance, and love in the face of our current situation, we continue to get a more accurate sense of where we are. Our GPS improves, locating us down to a square inch instead of a square mile.

Accurate requires a commitment to the other three aspects before it. Without honesty and acceptance, we're blind to what's going on around and inside of us. Without love, we're disconnected from our power to press onward.

The more accurate we can be in locating ourselves, the more clearly we can see the right next step along our path. And the more clearly we can see the next step along our path, the less that gets in our way.

Our location is constantly changing. You're going to continue reevaluating. And it's a virtuous cycle upward. Move, get data, reflect, adjust, move, get data. Rinse and repeat again if you'd like. Your client's hair will be delightfully clean.

STOP TRYING TO GET THEM SOMEWHERE

I know, I know. You want to provide value to your clients. You want them to get incredible results, change their lives, and change the world. You want them to stop getting hooked so often! You want them to have a breakthrough on every single call and weep tears of joy, release, love, gratitude, inspiration, and beauty. You want them to tell everyone they know about your work so you can do it over and over again with more people.

We become coaches to help people move forward. Our clients want results, and we want to help them achieve results. We can't ignore that part.

Accountability is good. Measuring progress is good. But stop needing them to get somewhere. Stop trying so hard to help your clients move.

They'll move when they're ready. You support them in the way they need to be ready.

THEY'RE RIGHT ON TIME

Everything in the Universe has unfolded perfectly to bring you and your client to this exact moment. They couldn't have changed anything even if they wanted to.

Going forward, they're right on time, too.

Their beliefs are going to shift exactly as quickly as they're going to shift. Their body is going to heal as quickly as it's going to heal. Their survival mechanisms and ego are going to hold on exactly as long as they're going to hold on. They'll expand on time and they'll contract on time. It might take only a moment for everything to shift. Hold that as a possibility with your client. And it might take longer. Too much or too little is a comparison against a reality that doesn't exist. It's all unfolding as it will.

Your job is to remember to unhook yourself when you forget, and to invite your clients to offer themselves that same gift.

Just this, just now. Right here. Right on time.

"THAT MAKES SENSE"

Three of the most powerful words a coach (or human) can use. It does make sense! Everything your client has done from the start of their life until today makes complete sense. Every step they took was in perfect alignment with their world.

Find the perspective from which their whole life makes sense. Find the place from which they don't need to go anywhere. You don't have to stay exclusively there — it wouldn't serve them much if you did — but know that you can access it.

Be the first person in the history of their life who doesn't need them to change one iota of who they are. Create a space into which they can relax fully and let everything down. Love every inch of their being and magic will happen.

You won't have to push or force or try to do anything. They'll do it on their own once they've stopped fighting to keep their armor up, once they've unhooked, and once they know you don't need them to be different.

They want to move forward. And they want it to come from their own unique expression, on their own timing and terms.

If they're not ready yet, that makes sense!

Try it out. Today, even. Go find a stranger and watch them in the world. Decide that everything they do is right and love them for it. Even (and especially) when it makes no sense to you, allow yourself to fully understand what they do.

Notice anything inside of you that shifts. Notice what you have to pick up or let go of. Flex this muscle often, as if you were working it out at the gym.

HONEST VS. REALISTIC (PART TWO)

We're here again, talking about being honest. At this point, your client might have some voices popping up telling them to be realistic, that they should be further along by now. Invite them back to honesty. *Back here, right now.* Look honestly at where they are, including their successes, growth, and trajectory. Check back in with their What For and desires.

With honesty comes power. It's completely okay to be here. And what else is calling them?

YOU CAN'T LEAVE A PLACE YOU HAVEN'T FULLY BEEN

Where are we right now?

Get used to asking that. If you're like me, you'll assume you know. Often as a coach, I don't. I know where I think my client is and where I feel pressure to move them toward. Beyond that, I'm guessing where they are.

Slow down to glimpse the full picture. Breathe it in. Every moment is new. Whatever is here is great. Touch the moment together and it'll shift all on its own.

"I'M HAPPY WHERE I AM"

That's okay. In fact, as a coach, I love this! It means my client has chosen to get off the roller coaster of searching for something wrong with their life. At first, this can be disorienting for them. They aren't quite sure what to do with the extra energy.

This part used to scare me as a coach. If they weren't striving for something, what if they no longer needed me? There must be something wrong! You might not do that, but I certainly have. The more I let go of my own fear and insecurities, the more I realized that this was when soul work can really begin.

There is a quietness in our client's mind and being when they're here, and that quiet allows for new things to emerge, along with a new clarity about them. It's like the clouds have cleared and we can see up the mountain for the first time.

126

The truth is, everything is okay! It always has been. When we remember that, we can finally breathe. It's like removing a 1,000-pound weight from our backs.

Celebrate being here. Slow down and track what this experience is like for them. What do they notice about this place of feeling content? What is different? What is the same? How are they relating to themselves, your work together, and the world around them?

As Loch Kelly invites us to consider, "What's here now when there's no problem to solve?"

THIS IS WHEN THE REAL WORK BEGINS

When there is nothing left to fix, your client suddenly has choice about everything in their life. Nothing has to change so they gain agency to choose what to change and what to keep exactly the same. That's the start of freedom.

Once they've taken a breath and gotten used to the air at this new elevation, invite them to take stock:

- What did they dismiss as impossible before now?

- What felt too hard to even consider shifting but now is more available for them?

- What in their life are they tolerating as a 7 when it could be a 10?

Not because they need to look at any of these things. Because they get to. Because life is gently and insistently inviting them to make it their own.

And how could upgrading any of these things also be an experience filled with delight, wonder, and joy (or whatever it is your client wants)?

Roll up your sleeves. It's time to get to work. How fun!

REMEMBER THE GAME YOU'RE PLAYING

Now is a great time to reflect on the game you and your client have been playing. (Every day is a great time and I highly recommend making this a regular practice. But giving this extra attention when things are going great can give your client a new perspective.)

As you reflect, ask:

- What are the rules of the current game?

- How is your client relating to them, following them, or avoiding them?

- What's useful about them? What isn't?

- How have the rules of the game shifted things in your client's life?

- Are joy, fun, and ease emerging on a regular basis, or for the first time?

- What does it mean to win?

- Is winning built into the game or is it an impossible struggle?

- What is the point of the game, anyway?

- Have you reached the current game's natural end point?

- What's it like for your client to win?

- What's the reward?

If your client has won their current game, it's time to build a new one based on where they are right now. Don't forget, they're playing a game all the time. And if they don't consciously design it, the rules will be based on old habits. What might a game look like if it's designed when things are already great?

If your client has just reached a new level in their current game, it's time to reflect on the journey so far and how things are working for them. Maybe they've mastered the rules and want to play in a new environment or with new companions.

Invite them to design the next level for themselves in a way they can win.

Get clear before advancing to what's next.

IT ISN'T ABOUT PUSHING

A common misconception is that coaching is only about generating something with a certain energy or force behind it. Sometimes that's true. And it definitely isn't all coaching is about.

Coaching — like life — can be softer and subtler while remaining just as powerful. In fact, the moments in which there is no pushing can be the most powerful.

For the first two-plus years of our relationship, that's how my partner related to coaching. She always brushed it aside as something she'd look into when she wasn't so full with other things. (Ever heard that from a client before?) For her, coaching meant adding something extra. It was a top-down force imposing something upon her, and with it came the burden of expectations. That's how many of us relate to creating a vision and setting goals. But it isn't a requirement.

Possibilities opened for her after we worked with a relationship coach for a few months. She started to realize that the weeks in which she didn't have anything pressing could be the most transformative for her.

Once she stopped needing to get somewhere, what was available to her suddenly expanded. The desire for structure emerged, toward activities that interested her. More passions and curiosity began to flow.

It's like acclimating to a new elevation. Sometimes we just need a second to catch our breath and admire the view. There is no rush.

What happens when your clients allow what's next to emerge on its own?

HOW GOOD CAN YOU LET IT GET?

Gay Hendricks' book *The Big Leap* popularized the idea of upper limits — the threshold we've unconsciously put into place for how much joy, money, success, love, connection, and overall goodness we allow in our lives — and the ways we sabotage ourselves when we hit them. Befittingly, friends told me to read the book for a couple of years before I finally did and was able to grasp the amazing extent of this phenomenon.

(I've been known to preemptively self-sabotage. It's a cute trick.) And once I saw it, I couldn't unsee.

There is a version of each of us open fully to the love the world wants to offer us. That's true for you, me, and your client. If we choose to let it in. Your client might not be ready to receive the gifts of your service. That doesn't mean you don't offer them.

Everything is perfect in this moment. How much can they let in? How much can you let in, even when they've hit their limit? How good can it get for both of you?

Opens arms up as wide as they'll stretch

This good!

RINSE AND REPEAT (PART TWO)

This might be where you start to feel a pull to rush forward. You and your client are super excited. You're clear on where they're going, you've practiced identifying where they are right now.

They're allowing for more and more of what they want in their life. Next stop: the moon.

That's great. Now slow down again. Stay in the process.

Check in again. Where do they see the two of you right now, in this moment? What is their perspective on the conversation? What are the two of you looking at? Where do they want to head?

As the Zen masters taught: Chop wood, carry water.

CELEBRATE THE GROUND TAKEN

Don't forget that your client is creating something impossible. As they move forward toward their vision, every step along the way is a step into new territory. It's expanding their world and opening a new reality.

Celebrate this.

It might be a new muscle for them (or you) to flex. It might feel uncomfortable or wrong. It might bring up feelings like guilt or shame or fear. They might have stories about what it means to let themselves win, even a little, along the way. That's more grist for the mill. It's information to get more honest, accepting, loving, and accurate about where they are right now. How it's going right now is likely how it will go anytime they undertake a new goal.

If they insist on making it hard and painful, devoid of celebration, invite your client to consider whether that's the game they want to play. Support them in distinguishing between their current experience and the one they actually want. Then celebrate that.

What if streamers and dance parties were allowed at any point along the way? What if celebrating didn't mean stopping our progress but was a vital part of moving forward, like rocket fuel for getting places faster?

This can *all* be fun. It can *all* be the best part of the journey. They simply have to choose for it to be so.

BREAKDOWN CITY

At some point — even when your client practices unhooking, even when they can celebrate and acknowledge the ground taken, even as they get better at honestly and accurately locating themselves — their current strategy for operating will become unworkable.

They'll see that their current context doesn't allow them to take the next step forward. They'll witness the things they believed were true about the world falling apart in front of their eyes. They'll understand that the hammer they keep picking up won't help them remove a screw from the wall (at least not without collateral damage).

They'll see all of this. And they won't know yet what to do instead. They'll be in breakdown.

UNDERSTANDING BREAKDOWNS

Your client's life, which worked perfectly for them based on what they were already doing and what they already believed, has been upended thanks to the new vision they've set. Everything that made perfect sense before no longer fits into this new, expanded world. You're shutting down their old perfect system in order to create something new, and that results in some things being upset while they rebuild.

Think about it like a busy intersection. As your client began the process of transformation, they had an idea of making some part of their life better. It's like they had an intersection with stop signs and wanted to change it to a roundabout to let more cars through. With your support, they began breaking the system that was built to work one way. At first, there might be construction that shuts the entire intersection down. And then, people might be unsure of how to navigate it — where to look, how slow to go, when to get off.

One step at a time.

In the middle of the change, things will feel slower and more frustrating than at the beginning. It will even be "broken" for a time. That's what we call a *breakdown*. By the end, though, traffic will move much more quickly and with fewer accidents.

That's a *breakthrough*.

Breakdowns are like being hooked. But they feel much bigger while we're in them. Breakdowns simply mean that something isn't as it should be, or it is as it shouldn't be. It means life isn't working how they want it to.

Breakdowns are a normal part of the transformation process. As coaches, we intentionally invite people to dance on their personal edges in service of them creating their (currently impossible) vision. Just the act of asking what else is possible is confronting to their current reality. For safety, your client's ego will fight against change and deny that anything outside of their current world is possible. It's a good thing you're around to keep inviting the question.

To create a new way of being (transformation), their old way of doing things has to stop working. From there, they can rebuild.

HOW WE RELATE TO BREAKDOWNS

Many of us relate to breakdowns as being *in the way* of where we want to go. If they weren't there, we could get to where we want to go without any trouble. From that perspective, we can hold them as annoying or frustrating or something to avoid. When the intersection is closed for construction, it's difficult to see the future benefit of having a roundabout in place of stop signs. We want it functioning now! So, we decide we should avoid construction altogether.

From that perspective, our clients will do anything they can to avoid their breakdowns. They'll habitually repeat the same patterns that keep them stuck in place, never transforming.

That makes sense. Construction sucks! Another (and I assert, more empowered) way to relate to breakdowns would be to see them as simply being *on the way* to where we want to go.

The purpose of an intersection is to allow traffic from two crossing roads to flow efficiently and effectively. A roundabout is more effective at achieving that purpose than stop signs, and a bit of construction is a part of transforming the intersection to meet that purpose.

After the breakthrough, way more traffic flow is available. In coach speak, more possibility is on the other side.

COACHING BEYOND BREAKDOWNS

As humans, we can tend to put a whole lot of significance on a breakdown — make it mean that something is wrong with others, the world, the coaching container, or ourselves — because it challenges our normal way of interacting and engaging in the world.

Normally, when stuff is broken, we rush to fix it and stop it from breaking again.

As a coach, it's important that we remember breakdowns simply tell us something isn't working. It's our responsibility to avoid personalizing, internalizing, or catastrophizing it. We have to maintain ground for the sake of the client's growth. And we need to remain open to the area of growth available from any breakdown.

Spoken differently: If masterful coaching requires us to increase our capacity to *be with* more, by necessity that means being able to be with our clients in the midst of their breakdowns. Remember, coaching is a spiritual journey. When you signed up for this, you signed up for breakdowns as part of the deal.

Sometimes this means taking responsibility for things that aren't ours. Sometimes it means holding space while things aren't working. Sometimes it means repeatedly pointing at old habits as they come back. It always means trusting that our clients are exactly where they need to be and that they have all that they need to make it to the other side.

Breakdowns are a part of growth.

BREAKDOWNS IN THE COACHING ITSELF

At some point, your clients will likely blame you for their breakdown. You'll invite them to a larger vision. They'll jump in, start taking action, and — at some point — fear or resistance will show up, shaking their confidence and inviting them back into old patterns.

For many of us, those patterns include blaming something in our environment. And guess what's new in their environment, ripe for finger-pointing? You.

That's okay. I won't go so far as to say it's expected because I don't believe every client needs to break down to realize success. But it is completely normal. Your work is confronting your client's concepts of expectations, disappointment, agency, possibility, and their internal state.

THE HYPE CYCLE

You might be familiar with the Gartner hype cycle. It's a curve that demonstrates cultural responses to new technologies. A graphical representation is below. I find many new things in our lives — relationships, jobs, hobbies, moves, and coaching — tend to follow a similar cycle.

The new thing starts with a trigger. Your client identifies a new desire or pain. They meet you and have a conversation. They read a book about coaching. Something sparks action. Next, they hit the Peak of Inflated Expectations. (It's important that we capitalize it to demonstrate how much significance we tend to place on it.)

The Peak is possibility. It's your client seeing for the first time a new way of life is possible. It's the grand vision they set, their impossible goal, and the excitement that surrounds it. They're Dorothy singing and dancing on her way to the Wizard, before the flying monkeys and dark clouds appear.

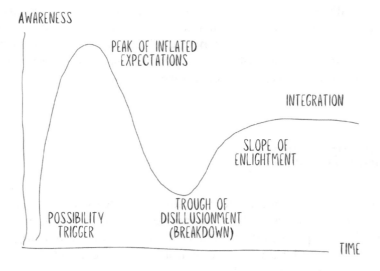

THE HYPE CYCLE

Download all of the illustrations and tools from this book at www.goldenbristle.com/bookresources.

THE TROUGH OF DISILLUSIONMENT AND REALITY

You can guess what happens next. Life hits. Fear shows up. Resistance rears its ugly head. They have some insights that feel good at first but, now, are just annoying because nothing seems to be changing. They adjusted some behaviors, and those adjustments aren't having the stellar results they'd hoped for.

This new thing must not be working. That's why they've learned to keep their expectations low. That's why they set goals they know they can attain or none at all, in case they don't want them after all.

Actually, yes, maybe they don't really want this new life. If they did, they'd be more disciplined or confident or feel more in flow every day. If only they believed in themselves more.

Something must be wrong.

This is when people quit. I know because this is when people quit with me. It used to happen some months into our work, as we slowly identified and worked toward their true desires.

These days, when it happens, it can happen much sooner. They're playing a bigger game and their old strategies melt away quickly.

YOUR CLIENT HAD NO CHOICE

This realization changed everything for me. It's easy for me to make my clients wrong in the midst of their breakdown. I see what's available to them if they simply stick it out. I see the beauty in what they're creating and the divine potential in them to bring it to life. How can they not see it?

Well, because they can't. Because their entire life led them to this moment and all of their beliefs, behavior patterns, and context for the world and what's possible are colliding in a perfect storm.

It had to come to this. And now their ego is going to fight to stay in the safety of their created world, even if it means attacking the thing supporting them in moving toward something better.

Your job is to see that, to gain the perspective from which their desire to quit is not only a perfectly rational choice but the only way this could have ended up right now. That gets you back on your client's side and, from there, you can see so much more.

When you realize they have no choice, you can hold them with compassion. When you can see how everything added up to this moment, you gain an honest and accurate perspective on where they are. When you can accept them without blame, you can invite them into a choice about what's next.

THERE IS ANOTHER OPTION

Even though they had no choice but to get here right now, going forward they do have another option.

Go back to the start:

- What do they want?

- What do they *really* want?

- Where are they choosing from desire versus should or being realistic instead of honest?

- Where are they right now?

- What is their honest, accepting, loving, accurate location right this moment?

- And what's the next step? (Not what you see for them. What *they* see for them.)

This is why they signed on to work with you. It's Neo choosing the red pill. Not the end of the journey or the fix for everything in their life. It's starting down the rabbit hole. This is where your work truly begins.

Their old pattern has appeared to show them what life is like if they continue to choose it. Likely, it's a really good life. It's worked for them until now. No shame in choosing that again.

You're here to invite them into something different in the face of that. It might not work. The road ahead hasn't yet been built. And it's what they want. The road behind has already been paved. Accept it. They have another option for the road ahead.

THE MICROCOSM BECOMES THE MACROCOSM

Often, the coaching relationship represents more than what we think it might as coaches. Our clients might make us their mother or father, their disapproving teacher, an idol or guru, or the sibling they never had. I won't debate the good/bad, or right/wrong of it. I'm merely pointing out that it is.

Your clients are bringing all the expectations they've gathered about how people will respond to them into your work. They have expectations about quitting, about how you'll handle conflict, about what their fear means for your relationship.

You get to love them through all of it. You get to help them engineer a new experience of being in breakdown. One they can carry with them everywhere in life. I know because I've experienced it as a client and a student.

In my Senpai training year of the Samurai Coaching Dojo, I struggled. My experience of my teachers (still dear friends, mentors, and colleagues) was they were mean, had impossible standards, wouldn't let me win, didn't give me proper instructions so I could succeed, and were setting things up so I'd fail. I felt angry and spiteful.

On one of the team calls, I shared my feelings, expecting to be told how wrong I was and to have them be defensive in return. Part of me was looking for punishment so I could be justified in my anger. Instead, I was met with calm love.

They invited me to go move my energy and return to the call so I could ask for what I needed. I wasn't kicked out (which was my fear) and they didn't engage with my anger. Instead, we looked at what was going on for me under the surface — the stories I had and the patterns from which they emerged — and I was invited to share my struggle with them.

142

I was included rather than excluded. I received safety rather than punishment.

It didn't fix things. It was still really challenging for me. But I no longer felt like my belonging was at stake. I had a new way of operating within these strong feelings, and a new system of support to grow into. And I could take that system to other relationships, learning to trust myself and others to meet me with love.

The work we do in our coaching container gets practiced outside of it. And our clients often use us to repattern relationship dynamics they formed a long time ago.

Your love for your client in your sessions is shared everywhere they go.

ON QUITTING

Sometimes you'll meet your client exactly where they are in a breakdown. You'll love them in their pattern. You'll support them in identifying a way through. You'll give them exactly the medicine you think they need in the moment.

And they'll still opt out.

That's okay.

It's heartbreaking (for me). It brings up feelings of all sorts. That's also okay.

SOMETIMES QUITTING IS THE RIGHT THING

It has to be. You're in the practice of living into each moment anew and trusting your client is exactly where they need to be. Quitting isn't separate from that.

There are a few insights I'm still integrating these days (maybe by the time you read this, I'll have brought them in fully). One is that not everyone is here to seek enlightenment, and that's okay. Even more, not everyone's path toward enlightenment is going to look like mine or like I imagine theirs should. And that's okay, too. Even more yet, both of these insights assume that I even have the faintest idea of what enlightenment looks like — or that it's a desired journey to take on.

Truth is, I don't know.

And neither you nor I know what's best for your client. Our job is to trust that they do while continuing to be a loving stand for what they say they want.

HANDLING YOUR STUFF

It's a pretty sure thing that you're going to have thoughts, feelings, and judgments about your client quitting. Even when you think you're all good, those thoughts may come back.

This is a friendly reminder about the importance of you working with your own coach. Let it all pass like a storm. Give it space to clear and heal. Honor what's there to be honored. Carry forward the lessons you learned.

And get clear again so you can get back at it, loving them and your other clients exactly where they are.

Drop back into the being of coach and go serve.

PART FOUR:

COACHING WHAT'S

IN BETWEEN

PART FOUR:

COACHING WHAT'S

IN BETWEEN

COACHING IS GPS NAVIGATION
PART FOUR: NAVIGATING THE ROUTE
IN REAL-TIME

ONCE WE'VE PUT in our current location and desired destination, our trusty GPS pops out an optimal route with step-by-step directions for what to do. Navigating life might not feel that simple or easy — some of your clients' goals might have more complexities than a mile-long trip to the gas station — but that doesn't mean we're without a similar set of tools for designing a route.

Remember, what your client is creating next is impossible in their current world. This means that you and they can put less pressure on crafting the perfect route. Instead, it's about crafting a route and adjusting based on the results.

This is where we can act like the navigation system. Break things down, turn-by-turn.

We'll talk more about creating the smallest next step. Define measurable results to guide which path to turn down next. Your client can become like my friend who sets their odometer at each step so they know how far they've gone.

On the personal growth journey, emotional snarls are like unexpected traffic backups. Sometimes they take patience while things calm down. Sometimes your client can turn their car into a flying machine and move around the broken-down cars along their path.

When you both continue keeping an eye on where they currently are, you'll have a better sense of what tools or companions they need to cross the next chasm.

Notice when you become a backseat driver and choose to allow your client to steer the way. Be curious about how you can be the best road trip companion possible.

And remember that it's quite helpful to look back at how far you've come to acknowledge the ground covered. Celebrate each state line you cross, giving thanks for where you've gone, and for what's ahead.

ON WHAT'S IN BETWEEN

By the time you've gotten this far, most of the work has been done. I know it's counterintuitive, but it's true. The process of identifying what they want, then getting clear on where they are right now has already opened your client's mind to new possibilities. The road ahead of them is visible because they have a destination. That's the hardest part. Now they're on track.

It's like there is a magical force pulling them forward. The more their attention and focus remain on where they want to go throughout each day, the more they'll naturally move closer on their own.

The more they're able to see their destination with respect to where they are right now, the more the next step will reveal itself to them. And the more they're connected to their What For and larger vision, the more energy they'll have to take that step, even when it feels risky.

WHAT'S IN THE IN BETWEEN?

What's in between where they are right now and where they want to go might be a whole host of things, including:

- The strategy, tactics, and routes they can select to move to where they want to get (including shortcuts)

- The new skills and tools they can learn to aid them on their path

- The beliefs, worldviews, and patterns that either add self-imposed traffic or clear the way for a smooth ride

- The new structures, systems, and habits that will help them make consistent progress

- The rest stops, milestones, and celebration markers to keep them fueled up

These are the same things you discover when you invite your client to consider what they want and where they are right now. You know how to do this!

IF YOU SKIPPED HERE, GO BACK

I know I told you there was no right or wrong way to read this book. That's true.

And.

Skipping to this section of the book without reading the first two parts is like your client grabbing at strategies before clarifying what they want. It's not bad. It's simply not as effective as slowing down and focusing on WHAT before HOW.

I know it's tempting. When I first started coaching, I wanted to get to the "coaching" part as quickly as possible. I wanted to produce shifts in my clients. I wanted to show them (and myself) that I was great. I was hooked. I made it about me.

You know better. Don't be the coach who runs around in circles with your clients. Don't go on fishing expeditions without being clear on what your client wants to catch. Don't get yourself hooked on needing to get somewhere, having a client cry or feel catharsis, or going straight to "deep work."

You're here to do something different. How? By not skipping to what you imagine is the good part. By, instead, being a stand for your client's wisdom and clarity. By being with them in their process of identifying WHAT before HOW. (Yes, I'm repeating. It's that important.)

If you haven't yet read and implemented the steps in the first parts of this book, stop now and go back. Take a breath. Love yourself like crazy. I certainly love you. Slow down. Be in the process.

For my chronic section skippers, I'll ask you where else that shows up in your life. What else are you missing because you insist on jumping ahead? This is not to say there is greater virtue in covering every inch of a topic. Instead, it is to say we all can benefit from being able to operate on every part of the spectrum. And I invite you to put in some reps on the side you don't often touch.

THE SECRET TO GETTING THERE

The secret to navigating what's between where your client is and where they want to be is right in front of their face:

Where to next?

That's it. A big, fancy plan isn't required. (Sometimes it helps.) They don't need to make a huge leap today or fix everything in their life. They need to do the next thing, to move to the next step along the path, and keep their eye on the final destination.

As I write this, I'm worried that this book is full of overly simple concepts. From the start, I've told you that's the case. Yet, they're also infinitely deep and nuanced. And when put together, they work. That fear also shows up for me as a client. I look to big, elaborate plans and can sometimes miss the simple move right in front of me.

Each of us has our own strategies and methods for avoiding the simple (often courageous) next move. Your job is to be with your client as they try to avoid them and to support them in coming back to what's real, taking the next step along the way.

Now, onto what's next.

REMEMBER: THIS IS A GAME

Your client is playing Chutes and Ladders (or Snakes and Ladders, or whatever you want to call it). Even better, they're playing the version in which they write the rules.

If they want to win every time, they get to. If they want everyone to play on the same team, it's their prerogative. They can teleport backward or forward or add shortcuts anytime. And they can take a break, too.

Play is the point. Discovery is baked in. They make up how it works. And their objective determines the design.

Now have some fun.

WHAT'S THE NEXT STEP?

Make this your third favorite question. Just like your navigator reveals the next move along your driving path, invite your client to find the next step for them.

Where to now, boss? What do you see?

Let them guide the way.

GO SMALLER AND SMALLER AND SMALLER

Ask your client what needs to happen for them to get to their target. If they're anything like me, they'll give you an answer that sounds like something from the Underpants Gnomes. (Google this if you don't know. I promise, it's worth it).

Without help from my coach, my marketing plan might look like this:

Phase 1: Collect LinkedIn connections

Phase 2: ???

Phase 3: Big profits

Look out for magical thinking. If there aren't enough steps to logically arrive at their target, they just need more steps. It's that simple.

Your client will probably try to fool you, telling you they have this part handled. You'll ask them if they're clear on what they're doing next and how it moves them forward. They'll assure you they are without much detail. Then they'll hang up, promptly forget everything you talked about, and feel overwhelmed by the massive goal in front of them.

Invite them to make their steps smaller. Like, stupid small. What's the tiniest action they can take to move something forward?

BJ Fogg, a Stanford professor and expert on habit building, instructs people to floss one single tooth if they want to start flossing. Why? Because it's super easy to say yes to one tooth. Then, once we've started, we'll likely finish the rest of our teeth.

154

What would flossing one tooth look like for your client? And how can they document and track it so that they win?

IF YOU COULD SHIFT ONE THING TO MAKE THE BIGGEST IMPACT, WHAT WOULD IT BE?

Sometimes we (meaning me, but also probably your clients) avoid speaking about the most important thing because we have certain feelings about it. It's scary or daunting or we have a story that it'll be hard to do. So, we (again me) focus our attention on things that don't actually move us forward. You know, like answering emails or checking Facebook instead of inviting that person I want to work with to a conversation. Answering emails isn't bad. It will lead somewhere. But the invitation to a potential client could change my life with far less effort.

This question cuts through all of that. If your client commits to answering it honestly, lovingly, and accurately, their wisdom will point them in the right direction. The best part is, the more they focus on the things that produce tangible wins, the fewer steps they'll have to take along the way. It's like choosing a road straight to their destination instead of making 16 turns in some random neighborhood.

HOW CAN YOU LET THIS BE [FUN]?

Or easy. Or exciting. Or adventurous. Or a super-splendiferous win-win extravaganza. Or whatever experience your client wants from this part of their game. How they move anywhere in their life is how they move everywhere. Now is the time to practice moving with intention, and living the life they want. Now.

Ask these questions of yourself and your clients:

- What experience do you want in your coaching?

- Do you want confidence and ease? *Great!*

- How can you allow for more ease in this moment?

- How can you open yourself to more confidence right now?

More than just helping them bring their desired experience to the here and now, this question opens your client's creativity. "Oh yeah," they'll say, "how might I do that?"

Let's explore. Expand their menu and their idea of what's possible will keep expanding, too.

IF YOU ALREADY KNEW THE ANSWER, WHAT WOULD IT BE?

You trickster coach, you. Calling forward your client's innate wisdom in the face of their resistance. Quite clever. Seriously, though, they do know. They always know. That's what I believe, at least. Your client might have *feelings* about the answer, however. Those feelings might appear to be in the way of them answering. That's okay. You'll simply address that when it's present, with love and compassion and courage. You know how to do that.

Teach your client to become a time traveler who can fast forward to their imagined future, then look back at the path that led them there. Help them practice being the person who's made it happen, embodying the energy the new version of them exudes, along with the wisdom they possess.

It's like being able to meet with a mentor who knows all the answers anytime they want. And this mentor is with them 24/7!

Even better, this question lets both of you off the hook. You as a coach don't need to know anything since your client already does. And they don't have to go digging around, researching, or wasting time looking for the answer because they already know it. It's a win-win.

Tool: The ultimate results formula

Here's a handy tool your clients are going to either love (if they crave structure) or hate (if they resist structure). Either way, I present to you the ultimate formula for creating and measuring results in your life.

Like the framework for coaching I've presented, it's quite simple. And some fun news: it's a lifelong game in which you control both the challenge level and whether you win or lose.

$$\textbf{(Goals + Structure)}$$
$$\textbf{x Environment}$$
$$\textbf{x What For}$$
$$\textbf{= Results}$$

Goals

Goals are the things we're shooting for. As we've covered, they're broken down into two things:

- tangible results

- and experience.

Tangible results = SMART goals. They're specific, measurable, attainable, relevant, and time-based. We know when we have reached them, and when we have not.

Generally speaking, the size and ambition of the original goal influence the rest of the equation. The larger the goal, the larger the available results. There is no moral or inherent value judgment in these statements. It's simply math. Remember, as your client learns to declare their goals, they'll also learn to remove their identity from the goals.

Having a smaller goal does not make someone less worthy and having a larger goal does not add to their worth as a human. It's simply a marker by which to evaluate:

1. realized results, and

2. the structure and environment required to meet such a goal.

Generally, a bigger goal requires improved structures and environments in order to achieve desired results.

Experience = how we want life to go for us as we're working toward the goal, and as it's realized in our everyday life.

It's one thing to make $1 million while working 18 hours a day and isolating oneself from friends and family. It's another to make $1 million while also having a rich social life and enjoying feelings of freedom and delight.

To most accurately and effectively evaluate our results, both the goal and experience need to be accounted for in equal measure.

Structure

Structures are the specific systems, habits, practices, tools, and operations that move us toward our goals. Again, larger goals generally require stronger structures alongside them.

I won't say "more systems" or "larger structures" because those aren't necessarily the answer. Sometimes simplicity is the optimal system for realizing certain goals.

Common structures include:

- journaling
- coaching
- meditation
- exercise
- team members (as this equation relates just as much to business results as it does personal results)
- daily schedules and to-do lists
- sleep
- SOPs (standard operating procedures)
- software tools and systems
- metrics dashboards
- and more...

Environment

Our environment has a multiplier effect on our results. It can either be a tremendous boost or a hindrance. I find that our environment is often either the most overlooked factor in our positive results or the most blamed factor in not achieving the results we set.

Environment is broken down into two aspects: internal and external.

Internal environment = the state of our mind, body, and spirit. It includes the way we talk to ourselves, the beliefs we have about the world around us, and the level of inspiration we find in our day-to-day life or our mission.

It also includes our physical health, including our strength, stamina, and energy level. Lastly, it includes our connection to something bigger than ourselves, and our ability to feel awe, wonder, grace, and gratitude.

External environment = the world we're in every day. It includes our physical space, the people we surround ourselves with, the quality of the Earth and nature around us, noise and light, the messages we're receiving, and the tools we have at our disposal.

Sometimes our environment can feel out of our control. We might believe that we can't leave behind people in our lives or leave the town we live in. We might also believe that our internal environment is unchanging, especially when we have feelings of anxiety or fear.

Whether you agree with those disempowered beliefs or not, it's important to understand that they are also a part of our environment. We cannot escape our environment and it's always influencing us. Part of realizing the results we want is becoming aware of our environment, then choosing to explore something different as a commitment to our goals.

The structures in our lives and our environment are intricately linked. One influences the other, and vice versa. Our environment (internal and external) affects our sleep, which affects our adherence to supportive structures like exercise, which affects our mental capacity, and on and on.

Choosing a support structure that upgrades our environment can have an outsized effect on our results because of the multiplier effect.

What For

Our What For is also a multiplying factor on our results. It's our driving force, our rocket fuel, the North Star that keeps us moving forward. We derive our What For from our purpose and commitment in the world.

As with the size of our goal, the power behind our What For necessarily determines the size of our results. Bigger doesn't mean better, but it does allow for more sizable results.

Without a compelling What For, we are likely to give up when life gets hard, or fall victim to a negative environment. We might end up achieving results we don't consciously seek because we're uncertain about why we're pursuing things in the first place.

Results

Results are simply what happens. They're the other side of the equation. Measuring and observing our results is a practice of evaluating the variables on the other side.

If we surpass our goals, we can look at the factors that created that result. From there, we can build upon our success and ask what we want in the future. And if we fail to reach the goals we had set out for, our results help us see which variables can be changed in the future to produce different results.

Sometimes it's as simple as changing the initial goal because we're happy with the results. (Yay!) Sometimes structures and environments need to be shifted if we want to remain committed to a bigger goal. As we move then adjust, previously unreachable goals become attainable.

Download all of the illustrations and tools from this book at www.goldenbristle.com/bookresources

WHERE DO YOU WANT TO GET TODAY?

As a client, I hate this question! Just ask my coach. I want to thrash and scream and demand my coach tell me where we're going. After all, I've already declared what I really want. Isn't that enough? Now coach me!

As a human committed to transformation, though, I love it. It brings up all of my stuff (and my clients'). It is a beautiful forcing function, revealing to us that there is no ground except for the ground we try to create ourselves. We're in the driver's seat. Where to now?

That's the source of this question's power. It reminds us, as clients, that we get final say. We get where *we* want. We decide if the work we're doing is useful, powerful, helpful, or meaningful. And if it isn't, it's on us to ask for something different.

Yes, it's another version of asking what your client wants. I told you that part is the majority of coaching. And just like the broader questions before it, the answer doesn't really matter. What matters is what emerges from it.

What does it reveal about your client's world?

They want clarity. Great! What for? What does it get for them? Not as a test. As a tool for understanding their motivations for action or context for change.

They want to identify the next steps. Great! What's their context for that? How does their system work for them now? What's the smallest step that would make the biggest impact?

They want to work through some feelings and judgments they're holding onto. Great! What opens up for them on the other side of that release? How does it connect to who they're a stand for being in the world?

166

Be curious with your clients as they're in the process of discovering what they want and they'll reveal their entire world to you. Get specific. Get curious. And invite them to choose the path.

HOW ARE WE DOING WITH YOUR REQUEST?

Again, this question is not a test. It's bringing you back to where you both are, based on where they want to go. You're inviting your client to ping their current location on the GPS:

- Are we on course?

- If not, where to next?

- What's missing?

The answer isn't about you! I know that sometimes I'm afraid to ask this question. What if I'm not coaching right? What if we're way off course? What if they're upset about that?

Well, there is only one way to find out. And finding out will help both you and your client recalibrate if something is off. Better to do that now than in three months when the wheels have completely fallen off the bus.

Ask this in every session. Heck, ask it multiple times. As you do, you'll both get to flex the muscle of locating yourselves in time and space. Even the times you don't align have the opportunity to bring you closer.

How do you relate to not being on the same page as your client? How do they relate? What's your default response? What's theirs? What magic is sparked for them by bringing all of that to light?

ON CONTEXT

Your client's context determines their life. The way they perceive themselves and the world around them, the way they relate to the events of their life, and how they choose to respond to them will directly influence their experience. This includes their context around coaching. And their context around goals. And their context around responsibility. And commitment. And on and on. Contexts are infinite in number. They're everywhere and all around us, largely invisible. Only when we begin to see them can we begin to shift them.

Become an expert at helping yourself and others distinguish contexts and you'll start to see transformation happen almost magically.

I could write an entire book distinguishing between the various contexts that run our lives. Short of that, here are two that will largely influence how your client relates to your work together and to the journey toward what they want.

AT CAUSE VS. AT EFFECT

Man, I really get annoyed when I'm in traffic. And when there are bad drivers around me. And when people hit their brakes unnecessarily. And, and, and, and, and...

In other words, I love to play the victim. I love to be at the effect of the world around me, to allow it to dictate my thoughts, feelings, and actions. To be able to blame others when I arrive late or have a poor attitude. It lets me off easy.

It also limits what I can do. It stops me from showing up as my most powerful self. It stops me from creating my most audacious dreams and visions. It leaves me at the mercy of the external world for the successes or failures in my life.

Of course, I'm not the only one who plays this game. Your client does, too. Many of the roadblocks they discover ahead will be there simply as a result of their worldview. When some outside force is in their way, invite your client to consider whether they're being at cause for their life or at effect of it.

- When they're *at effect*, they're the victim. The world acts upon them, placing obstacles in their way, and their only choice is to react against it. Barriers are exactly that and cannot be moved. Results are based on the happenings of the world at large.

- When they're *at cause* for their life, they're empowered to make the world they want. They and the world act in tandem, designing and creating a reality of their choice. Barriers (if they exist at all) are opportunities to find a creative solution. Results come from clarity, commitment, and action.

As you support your client in distinguishing the areas of their life in which they're feeling at effect, head back to the master question with them again.

What do you want?

Look for what feels impossible. Look for hedging based on what might be available versus true desires. Look for predicting and managing. Then invite them to something different — a new context in which they can be the cause of something better.

Once you return, the road ahead might look clear where it once had a host of obstacles along the way.

IN THE WAY VS. ON THE WAY

Your client is like Dorothy traveling along the yellow brick road. Along the way, they're going to meet scarecrows and tin men, lions and flying monkeys. There are going to be curves and hills. They can't get to the Wizard without crossing paths with each of these things. How they relate to them will determine how their experience of the adventure goes and their results along the way.

When we relate to something as being in the way, it's a roadblock. It's a problem that usually cannot be solved. We decide we can't get where we're going because there is a red light along the path.

It's similar to being at effect of the conditions around us. We're likely to stop before we ever get going because we're afraid something is going to block us partway.

When we relate to something as on the way, we're Dorothy making friends and facing our fears. When I drive somewhere, I accept that there are turns along the way. One road has a lower speed limit than others. Those things aren't impediments to me getting to my destination. They're part of the journey.

I join a Tough Mudder because of the obstacles, not in spite of them. So, when I get to the climbing wall that requires me to team up with others to scale it, I don't quit. I find someone to help me and I offer help in return. Things on the way become chances for us to grow, gain new skills and allies, and earn experience for the road ahead.

Most of the things that are both in the way and on the way of your client's journey are self-created. When they find themselves stuck or confused, invite them back to the basics:

- What do you want?

- Where are you now?
- What's the next step? Make it smaller.
- How can you let this be easier?

Slow down. Catch your breath. Then attack that wall to see what's on the other side. They'll be stronger and more capable once they do.

WHAT'S YOUR AGENDA?

I hope I'm not the first one to break this to you: You have an agenda. You want your client to succeed. You want them to be happy and healthy and realize their goals. You want them to find value in the work you do together. You want them to get somewhere in your sessions.

All the training and learning you've done as a coach is in service of that agenda. You're reading this book in service of that agenda. (Thank you.) No matter how much practice you've done, that agenda shows up with you when you're with your clients.

It's okay. It's human. Acknowledging it makes it possible for you to set it aside. Pretend it isn't there and you'll find yourself hooked on a regular basis.

ARE YOU GIVING THE DIRECTIONS?

Since you've made it this far in this awesome book, I'm going to make an assumption that you're intelligent, educated, and stick with things. You've probably had success in life. You have great ideas, make solid plans, and problem-solve well. Maybe you became a coach because you see things others don't and have a perspective you want to share in the world.

Your client may have hired you because of your expertise in a certain area or because you're an expert on a subject they're pursuing. They probably trust and seek out your opinion when they're feeling uncertain.

All the above can be a dangerous combination for a coach. Your ability to see around corners and build strategies for your clients might help them make progress in the short term. But, over the long run, it will stop them from building those capacities in themselves.

You aren't their GPS. They are.

Letting that happen is your work as a coach.

GIVE UP THE WHEEL

Your job is to stay on the lookout for whenever you think you know the right answer, want to offer a shortcut, or are attached to them moving in a certain direction.

And then, stop being right.

Go unhook and reconnect with your client exactly where they are. (Re-read Part three if you need to.)

Oh, and stop being wrong, too. You don't have to beat yourself up for having an opinion and getting hooked. It doesn't serve you or your client. You can't help but have an agenda. Let that go.

Drop back in. Put your attention back on your client. Get curious again. Look for their divine wisdom. Trust they'll find the right answer for them. Return to the energetic being of coach.

Be a stand for their greatness and your own.

Be everlasting light that pierces the darkness of fear and doubt.

Be the opening that allows them to realize their immensity.

Yes, you have an agenda. We all do. Now set it aside and go to work.

What is there for them to discover?

PLAY DUMB

This can be the one place in your life in which you don't need to know anything. Give the part of you that always needs to have an answer a break for the moment. It's always there if you need it, so no need to worry.

Let yourself be dumb.

Ask your client what they think they should do. Ask them what they are noticing. Be Buddy the Elf and let everything be a joyful discovery. *How fascinating! How fun! I wonder what will happen next?*

Playing dumb doesn't mean checking out. Stay fully with your client and your intuition. Feel your client, yourself, and the space. Keep attuned to every moment. Then simply let go of putting meaning on it or directing things.

Allow yourself to be surprised and who knows what magical things might emerge.

YOU'RE A BEACON

Your client signed up to work with you because they believe in their innate power and higher wisdom. Your conversations sparked something inside of them that had them believe they could transform. They embarked on this journey so they could let out a part of them that's been trapped inside until now.

Call them home.

Be a lighthouse that leads your client's divine clarity back to shore. Build a container that welcomes them and invites them to show up with everything they've got. Invite everyone to the party.

Tell them, "I see you. You can't fool me into believing you're smaller than you are any longer. No more tricks."

Then break all the rules and go play.

PLAYING WITH ENERGY

What your client creates or allows **room** for in a coaching conversation is the same thing they'll **create** in their life. Said differently, if your client is saying they want life to feel easeful and free, but they're making everything a slog in coaching, things won't be different outside of coaching.

You're dancing with them on the edge of their comfort zone. Fear is around but that doesn't mean it has to be frightening. Masterful coaches can play with the energy of the moment and transform it at their will.

Allow yourself to remain a spectator of the show while you're inside of it. Pay attention to the rules they've made up about how they're supposed to step. Feel and watch their body language to notice where they're loose and where they're tight.

Keep a close eye on the parts they decide need to be a grind and those that are allowed to be fun. Where do they lose the flow of the music? Where are they most in the groove?

It's all a dress rehearsal for life outside of coaching. How can they act as the person who's already living the life they want and already realized the goals they're moving toward, bit by bit, in your time together?

Be the court jester who can bring a key moment of levity to an otherwise weighty room. Be the fire-breathing magician who can enter and shift attention with a wave of your hand. Be the shaman who bops them on the head to wake them up to the life calling their name.

SEND THEM OFF INTO THE WORLD

Someone smart once told me that the three parts of coaching are to get your client, coach your client, then leave your client. We've done justice to the first two. Now, some attention on the third.

In some ways, being a coach is like being a parent and watching our kids go off on the first day of school. We've both done our parts to prepare. Now it's on them to put it all into practice.

Lots of coaches get hooked here, just like lots of parents get hooked. What if our work wasn't powerful enough? What if we missed something? What if they had just kept up with their gratitude journal? What if we had just challenged them on that one thing?

But our clients aren't our children. And worrying about all of that isn't our job. Our job is to get unhooked; to be reminded of their divine wholeness, wisdom, and power; to remain in integrity with our agreements; and to be the support they need to grow along the path they've chosen.

At some point, the work for right now is done. Just as it's done here. Any longer and I'll be writing for me and not you.

Off you go. Bon voyage.

PART FOUR: COACHING WHAT'S IN BETWEEN

PART FIVE:

WHAT'S NEXT

COACHING IS GPS NAVIGATION
PART FIVE: WHERE TO NEXT?

THE FINAL DESTINATION might never be final, and it will likely keep changing along the way. That's okay. We don't win by getting to the finish. That's not the point. But you know that by now.

What's next for me in this journey as a coach is to soften and deepen.

A friend once described his love for Joshua Tree in the fact that it goes on as far as the eye can see, looking the exact same. We can be miles down the path and have the sense that we haven't moved at all.

That's how coaching often feels for me. It's returning to old lessons over and over again, always a little different, hopefully a little wiser.

I believe the same to be true for our clients. They might let go of old directions once they're complete, but they'll also retain the skills they gained along the way. Our job is to meet them wherever they are along the path, no matter how defined their destination may be or how long a journey is ahead of them.

We're an invitation for them to choose their path powerfully.

You're an invitation.

I see you.

They've got this.

You've got this.

WRAPPING UP

This is the encore, one final gift for sticking around until the end. And I'm writing it just for you.

At the beginning of this book, I told you that I think coaching is a big fucking deal. I also shared with you my vision for a world in which everyone utilizes the skills and being of a coach. That's a very precious dream to me. It comes from the most tender part of my heart, as does this message.

Thank you.

Thank you for being courageous enough to raise your hand and declare that you also want to be a part of that vision.

Thank you for taking a stand for the possibility within all of us, rather than for our weaknesses.

Thank you for doing the crunchy human work of healing your own wounds so you can be of service to others.

Thank you for walking the path of a coach, even when it's dark and scary and full of weird noises and ominous shadows.

Thank you. You know not what you do.

And all that stuff I said is true about your clients — that they're infinitely wise, full of light, immensely powerful, and the like — that's all true for you, too. All of it. Every word.

Even on your bad days, or when you doubt yourself, or when you make a big mess. Even when you forget it. It's still true.

We need you.

We need your voice and your insight and your genius out in the world. Someone is just waiting for you to say the thing they need to hear so they can start their journey of transformation. Give it to them. Shoot, maybe I need it. Share it with me.

Keep going.

I know how alone you can feel sometimes walking this path. You aren't. I'm here with you. Others are here with you, too.

We'll feed you when you need it, just as you'll feed us. And as we move forward, we'll attract others. I know because I've seen it. And I know you've seen it as well.

It's time to wake up.

Let's go.

Love.

Matt

PART FIVE: WHAT'S NEXT

THIS IS COACHING

ACKNOWLEDGEMENTS

WOW. I NEVER THOUGHT this would be the hardest part of the book to write. The truth is, everyone I've ever met has contributed in some way to this piece of work. To anyone I've ever had the pleasure of calling a friend, teacher, or benefactor, thank you. Some people have played a more direct role in the preceding pages and with them, I will start from the start.

My parents taught me more than I could ever offer thanks for. Through their lives, I got to witness courage, love, strength, and resilience in action. Though I'm an idea guy, as I told my dad when I was young, I think I picked up some of their grit along the way. My family has always believed I can do anything I put my mind to, even if they haven't always understood what exactly my mind was doing. I'm eternally grateful for their openness to my kooky ideas and strong stances on just about every topic under the sun. I hope this book makes them proud.

The teachers I've had over the years never let me off easy, inviting me deeper into my own process many times over, and I'm all the better for it. They taught me that being smart isn't worth much if it isn't accompanied by kindness, humor, and perspective. May every student receive such lessons.

One December day in 2014, I decided I was going to create a more mindful world. Thank you to my friends who told me they believed I could do it rather than that I was crazy (no matter what they actually believed). Mike, Natalie, Kristin, Kelsey, Rob[2] — I wouldn't have stuck it out if not for your support. A few weeks later, I met Ksanti Maria at my first formal meditation training. She saw me (like really saw me) and invited me to fully play the game I might otherwise have tiptoed around, volunteering to be the mentor I never would have had the courage to ask for.

Karman put her faith in me and asked me to run a workshop for her brilliant Morehead Cain Foundation students and for that opportunity, I'm deeply indebted. That weekend inspired my TEDx talk and the Mindful Leadership framework that resulted in my first coaching clients. Speaking of my first clients, they're some of the smartest, most humble, generous, and powerful people I've ever met. I'm still amazed I had the chance to support them as a young coach. The same is true about everyone who trusted me as a coach-companion on their journeys of growth and transformation. I feel tremendously honored to have had the opportunity. This book exists thanks to their courage, love, and commitment.

Once I started to own being a coach, I grabbed a coaching time with Mike Harris who was doing a 50-conversation challenge. Mike sent me to *The Prosperous Coach* and suddenly everything sped up. (Rich Litvin and Steve Chandler wrote a seminal book on coaching so please read it if you haven't already.) Through Rich's community, I met Toku McCree and joined the Samurai Coaching Dojo. There, Toku, Christina Salerno, Adam Quiney, and Bay Leblanc Quiney were my first teachers. Their words are in so much of my writing these days that I fear I've straight up stolen them. When I refer to "my

ACKNOWLEDGEMENTS

coach," it's Bay I'm talking about. Her belief in me has kept me going when I've gotten in my own way over and over again. It brings tears to my eyes.

During the first year of the Dojo, I met Aaron Caulfield, Kevin Lawrence, Ted Riter, and others who have deeply informed who I am as a coach today. Ted became the first coach I hired (yes, a couple of years into my practice; don't be like me). He introduced me to the work of John Wineland and David Deida, and suddenly embodiment and sacred energetic forces were foundational parts of my everyday experience. (Being the mountain had no meaning for me before then.) In later Dojo years, I got to teach alongside some incredible master coaches — Dave Burns, Jesse Johnson, Ken Blackman, Greg Faxon, Hans Phillips, Bridgette Simmonds, Nicolette Routhier — all of whom I have borrowed from and hold dear in my heart.

Fate intervened to bring me to Kari Sulenes and Pilea from multiple directions. It's uncanny to meet someone with such a similar mission for the world and a shared drive to make it happen. Kari, Lisa, Jake, Howie, and their growing team are changing the world. It's a joy to learn from them and other incredible coaches in the Pilea network. Sandy Taylor, Brandon Houston and others, I'm looking at you and busily taking notes on all the mind-opening insights you share. I'm excited to learn and grow alongside each and every one of you in the years to come.

Lastly, a note to the wise, strong, magical wonder I get to call my person: Kristen. You see me when I can't see me, love me when I struggle to love me, and remind me that joy and play are always options for us to choose. I'm excited to make the impossible possible for and with you and to see where this grand adventure continues to take us. Thank you for reminding me that this book is a big deal even when I tell myself I should have another two written by now. More than anything, thank you for picking me. Your commitment to me, us, and everyone you love keeps me inspired to grow alongside you. Let's keep having fun.

ABOUT THE AUTHOR

Photo credit: Rob Symonds

MATT THIELEMAN is a transformational coach, visionary, speaker, advisor, and author. Matt works with leaders and change-makers to help them live into their purpose more fully, and bring their masterpieces to the world. He educates and trains coaches to be world-class in their field, and help their clients reach their full potential.

Prior to becoming a coach, Matt was in the marketing world, working with clients in practically every industry imaginable. There, he had a good look at how well-intentioned leadership not getting out of their own way was causing businesses harm. Matt has been a leadership coach since 2016 and spent 2021 as CEO of Pilea, a coaching organization for venture-backed founders. He is also a TEDx Speaker on the topic "Why The World Needs Mindful Leaders."

Matt lives in Colorado with his amazing partner, Kristen, where they enjoy everything the sunshine and mountains have to offer.

LET'S CO-DESIGN

YOUR GAME

IF YOU WANT to get on with changing the world together, I've designed some games for us to play.

I work with visionaries and leaders (if you're reading this, you're a leader) who are here for more than what following the normal path gets them, and ready to stop living the life they thought they were supposed to live — that winds up empty no matter how much they accomplish — so they can make the impact they're here to make.

If you believe in creating the impossible and bringing your soul's work to the world, or if you're a coach supporting others in that vision, come play.

www.GoldenBristle.com

The world is waiting. Let's get started.

—Matt Thieleman

Made in United States
Troutdale, OR
12/31/2023